WITH WORDS WE WEAVE

Texas High Plains Writers 2021 Anthology: Challenges

Texas High Plains Writers

Cover by Ashlyn Parker
Book layout by Kim Black

ISBN: 978-1-7338621-4-1

First Edition: 2021
www.texashighplainswriters.com

In memory of Lauralea Stephens and Suzana Sandoval

CONTENTS

INTRODUCTION

B y the time you read this, the year 2020 will be history, surely logged among the most chaotic in a generation.

But many of the stories that follow were written during the medical, societal, and political issues that gripped the world in what was supposed to be a year of celebration for the Texas High Plains Writers. Among the myriad events postponed or canceled last year was our centennial celebration, meant to honor the organization's formation on April 20, 1920, by Laura V. Hamner and Phebe K. Warner.

Though members were disappointed, the organization survived, as it has—without interruption—for more than 100 years.

The group changed, moving from in-person meetings to online gatherings, but the spirit and commitment never wavered, for adaptation is a trademark of the Texas High Plains Writers. Take the name, which has gone from Panhandle Pen Women to the Panhandle Professional Writers to its current designation.

Our story is inspiring.

It's little wonder, then, that the writers whose names appear in this anthology took the challenges they faced and spun them into inspired short stories and essays. Among them are *The New York Times* and *USA Today* bestsellers. You'll also find award-winning authors, mid-listers, and my personal favorite:

those whose words are appearing in print for the first time.

The anthology's theme is "challenges" for the obvious reasons, but the point was that we overcame those challenges, be them global or personal, and told the story.

And so we submit to you a collection that reflects the passion and grit that are synonymous with those who live, work, and write about our corner of the world.

Rick Treon
President, Texas High Plains Writers
www.texashighplainswriters.com

WRITERS BLOCK

Mike Akins

P ut up or shut up. They'll probably engrave that on my tombstone. Well, the chickens have come home to roost. I possibly—just maybe—might have run my mouth the last few years about how I could write a better book than that hack Nora Roberts.

Yeah, *that* Nora Roberts. *The New York Times* bestselling author of more than two hundred and twenty-five novels.

I do have a bunch of ideas—really good ones—for romance novels. But between you and me, I've not written a single durned thing since my days at A&M—unless you count the grocery list. I've written some great grocery lists in my time. My long-suffering husband, Earl—you'll like him once you get past the smear of Cheez-It's crumbs he proudly displays on every t-shirt—finally told me to get the typewriter out or shut the...

I won't bore you with the details.

Today's the day I put up, 'cause God knows I ain't ever gonna shut up. I throw open the closet door and stare daggers at this heap of junk threatening to spill out into the hallway. I know I've got an old Underwood typewriter in there some-wheres. Behind the TV trays and...

Why does any human being need so much crap? And it's not even my crap. Most of this stuff hasn't seen the light of day since we moved into the house ten years ago. I can hear Earl now: *You never know when you need to pull them lawn darts out to entertain!* Oh yeah, been a lot of them lawn-dart parties in the intervening years. You don't really want to be throwing them things with the kids around. Shoot, might as well hand out the steak knives and yell, *Get after it, boys!*

Where was I?

Oh yes, typewriter. I spy the case hiding behind the darts and the croquet set. Y'all really should come to the next back-yard barbeque, and I swear to God the darts and croquet set and corn hole boards are coming out! I might need to be drunk first.

I grab the handle of the typewriter case and yank and nearly pull my arm out of socket.

Sweet baby Jesus, is there a bowling ball in there?

I'd forgotten how much my grandma's old typewriter weighed. You gotta have a really strong conviction from the Lord about writing to want to drag this thing out on a regular basis. That's when I have my first *e-piph-an-y*. I tell Earl I need a word processor and he says, *What?* and I say, you know, a new laptop computer. Now, I've got a laptop, but you have to hand crank it to start it up. Y'all know I'm joking, right? He sets the box of Cheez-Its down and says something to the effect of, *Now, why in the…*

I won't bore you with the details.

Long story short, I promise if he gets me a new laptop I'll never mention writing again. Oh, and I might be playing lawn darts this weekend.

Earl and me and our two boys, Roy Dean and Buster, pile in the truck and drive out to the computer store. You've been to these computer stores, where there's fifty different kinds of laptops sitting out, anywhere from two-hundred dollars to two-thousand dollars. It's a little like potluck at the Baptist social. Them creamed corn casseroles look good, but one of 'em is gonna keep you up all night with a case of the trots.

Choose wisely.

I flag down the pale, pimple-faced boy who works at the

store and who looks like he lives in his parent's basement and I swear to God he's a vampire except it's broad daylight. He asks if I want a laptop for gaming or video processing, and I interrupt him and say, *Listen, I just want to write the next bestselling book.*

Pimple-face sorta slumps and mumbles about not needing a lot of RAM and how I don't really need a terabyte SS-something and some kinda I-69 processor or whatever it is and I interrupt him again and say, *I just want to turn it on and for it to work.*

He points at a shiny silver laptop that's three-ninety-nine. Earl about chokes and says he can buy a new shotgun for that much, when I remind him that *somebody* recently bought a two-hundred-dollar set of custom mud flaps and that shuts him up real quick.

I ask Pimple-face if I can word process on it and he tells me I'll probably want to get Word. No, they don't sell it, but I can download it. I tell Earl to remember *Word* and he sneers like he does when he gets pissy and says, *Word, word, word. I sure hope I can remember that! Word, word, word...* I am two seconds from snatching Earl bald headed except we're in public and I'm trying to model righteous living to Roy Dean and Buster.

Ignoring Earl, I ask if this laptop has email. Pimple-face looks like he might be having a stroke and through gritted teeth tells me this particular laptop comes specially equipped with email. What more can you ask for?

Fifteen minutes later we're headed home with my new laptop and I'm well on my way to becoming a *New York Times* bestseller.

Back in my little office, Earl and Roy Dean and Buster gather round like they're about to watch Neil Armstrong walk on the moon, and I fire the laptop up. It makes a bunch of cute little sounds and the screen comes up all colorful. Earl mumbles how he could've had a shotgun and he slinks off with his Cheez-Its and Roy Dean and Buster get bored and are off wrestling in the living room and I sit there with not a clue what I'm doing.

But, we all know great art is born of adversity.

Y'all, I sat there 'til I got a clue! I did one of them Google searches for Word. Did you know the Word program is not for free? I type in my credit card number and download Word, and I'm up and running.

I'm not sure what I was expecting. Considering I'm paying seventy dollars a year, I thought it would do more to help me write. Not to be dismayed, I pull up my big-girl panties and type in my first words.

    It was a

The cursor sits their flashing, waiting for my next turn of phrase, and all I can think of is *dark and stormy night.* Much as I'd like to channel the classics, this needs to be an original work. I backspace to the beginning and sit there staring at the screen. I hate to say it, but that blank page is awfully intimidating.

Well, inspiration struck and I pull up my big-girl panties again. I'm gonna start with my character name.

    Jane woke up and decided she'd go to the flea
    market today.

Should I use *flea market* or *swap meet*? Writing is tough, y'all. Anyways, I figured she'd meet her lover-to-be at the flea market. As I reread my sentence, I see another problem. Jane is too plain for a hot-blooded Southern girl. I need a name that's memorable, like Scarlett.

I fire up the Google and do a search for hot-blooded Southern girl names. I had no idea there were so many to choose from. Let's see: Annabelle, Caroline, Daisy…

Did you know, and I did not know this, that Annabelle comes from the Hebrew word for *grace* and the French word for *beauty*? And Daisy is from Old English meaning *day's eye* because the flower opens in the morning and closes at night. Did you also know you can spend hours looking at names and where they come from?

The afternoon is gone, and I only have the one sentence to

show for all my efforts. I need to get after it, but if I pull my big-girl panties up any further they'll be around my neck.

Earl shambles in to ask me when supper will be ready and I tell him one of these days they'll make enough Cheez-Its to stuff that hole of his full and he's says, *Hardy har, I guess today ain't that day.*

I power down my computer, slap together a fine Southern meal, and marvel—not for the first time—how anyone could shovel that many chicken fried steaks down their gullet on top of all them Cheez-Its. Tomorrow, I promise myself, I'm gonna knuckle down and get some writing done.

Next day, I'm up at the butt crack of dawn and sitting at my computer and I make a discouraging discovery. My whole novel—all one sentence of it—has disappeared. A complete day's work gone. I Google the problem and it turns out you have to save your document. There should be some kind of instruction manual on the ins and outs of writing. By this time the sun is well up, and Roy Dean and Buster shuffle in asking me to make French toast. I bet no one asks Nora Roberts to make French toast. Fingers poised over the keyboard, I tell them I'm busy and they whine about how they're starving and I tell them to go make their own damn French toast!

They run off, and I hear them telling Earl how I cussed at them. Then Earl's in my office moaning about how my writing career is throwing the family into a panic. I give him a look that could wither forty acres of wheat and now he's in the kitchen making the boys French toast. I hear cabinet doors slamming and pans banging and pretty soon something's burning and how on God's green Earth am I supposed to write a best seller with all this racket going on?

This is your classic case of writer's block, if you don't already know.

Time for a little therapy to get the creative juices flowing again. I grab my credit card, and before Earl can say *boogedy*, I'm out the door and on my way to Dillard's. A little shopping does wonders for organizing your thoughts, and there's nothing quite like a new pair of slacks or a cute little dress to make you feel like a productive human again. I diddle around the store for a bit when my eye falls on this absolutely adorable Coach shoulder bag for only three fifty. Girl, ain't no better therapy than a new purse.

I reach for it same time as this other lady, and we both latch on and the tug of war commences! She has fifty pounds on me, but my writing escapades have pushed me to the brink, and I'm loaded for bear. With a primal snarl, I dig in both high heels, flex my glutes, and strain so hard I feel like I'm about to give birth.

My mortal enemy grits her teeth and sets her Birkenstocks, cheeks puffed out, arms shaking with effort. We lock eyes and the prize see-saws back and forth. She turns redder than a Beefsteak tomato and I feel the strap slip in her hands, just a smidge, but enough that the fear comes over her.

With a final furious heave, I wrench the purse free. Birkenstock stumbles backward, scattering racks of belts and hats to the four winds as she cartwheels to the ground before coming to rest, arms and legs splayed like she's doing the breaststroke. I lift the purse over my head, and I'm Rocky Balboa hoisting the world championship belt, blood and sweat pouring off my face. Adriannnnn!

This mousy little man is at my side. His name tag says Manager, and I look him up and down and calmly say, *I believe I'm ready to make my purchase now.*

I drive home like one of them people in *The Fast and the Furious*, which is what I do when I'm amped up. Nobody got killed, so no harm done. I park in the driveway, only I can't bring my purse in the house without getting the third degree. But now my creative juices are flowing again, and I know exactly what to do; I'll hide it on the back porch and sneak it in later.

I throw open the back gate and I'm running across the lawn. You know, it's hard to run in high heels on a good day. Well, Earl had just watered the grass and my left heel punctures the ground like one of them lawn darts and I went flying like Birkenstocks did back at the Dillard's.

Long story short, I broke my left ankle.

Earl was pissed, both about the Coach purse and the ankle, but this story has a happy ending. First, I'm not playing lawn darts this weekend. Second, I can't do any cooking or housework for a while, so Earl and Roy Dean and Buster will have to manage without me. I'm propped in front of my laptop and I finally have some time to write.

Daisy.

I've decided that's the name of my character. Watch out, boys! She's headed to the flea market and she's going to kick some ass. And then, she's going to fall in love. Come to think of it, that's pretty close to how Earl and I met.

Mike is a computer programmer and past president of the oldest writing group in the state of Texas—Texas High Plains Writers. When he's not practicing an obscure style of Okinawan karate, he can be found in front of his laptop banging out the next *New York Times* bestseller (one of these days). He loves Fantasy and pretty much any genre that's well written. If you corner him and ask him about writing or karate, expect to get an ear full!

REMNANTS OF HER

Kim Black

"**D**o you remember when we were kids on Robin Hood Drive, and we would ride our bikes on the bridge over the creek by our house?"

"I remember the stories you tell me, Mama." I'd heard them hundreds of times.

"Remember the time that big monitor lizard sat right in the middle of the bridge, and we had to wait until he crawled away? We were scared because he was so big. I'll bet he was five feet long." Mama raised her silver-white brows high. "He was like a dragon. You were scared of him, too, weren't you?"

I nod and smile. "I'm sure I would have been. I jump at the little six-inch lizards in my backyard now. I don't think I'd be brave if I came face to face with a five-foot-long dragon."

She laughs. "It wasn't a real dragon. But Vince and I were scared. You remember?"

This was the part I hated. The moment I resented. "Well, Mama." I emphasized *Mama*. "I'm your daughter, and you were just a kid. I wasn't born when you lived on Robin Hood Drive."

The deep crease forms on her forehead and tracks down between her brows. Her smile vanishes. Her fingers begin their dance—flexing and curling around each other. She frets over what she said wrong. No matter how many ways we start a conversation, it always seems to come to this point. "You're not Sue?" She studies my face, finally shaking her head. "Are you April?"

"No, Mama, I'm not either of your sisters. I'm your oldest daughter."

A flash of recognition. "Oh, yes. I forget sometimes. Your dad calls it—I can't remember the name of it. But it's a disease in my brain. Makes it so I forget things sometimes."

"I know. But it's okay. You remember the important things." But for how much longer?

"I love my little sister. She's just a baby, compared to me." Her face turns placid, back to vivid memories. "I was a teenager when she was born. She was like a doll to me." I anticipate her next question. "How old is April now?"

I do the math. "She's sixty-one."

Mama's brow furrows again. "That's not right. She's younger than me."

I nod. "Yes, but, Mama, you're seventy-four."

She wrings her hands again. The numbers confuse her. I search the room for anything to draw her attention.

"Where did Dad take you yesterday? He said you were going for a drive."

The new topic settles into her eyes, and she smiles, if only for a moment. "We went out to see the lake. But there were too many people, and we didn't have a picnic. We used to have picnics, but not anymore. I can't get up and down from the ground. It hurts my knees. So we just get drive-up food and sit in the hot car. It's not too fun, but it doesn't hurt my knees."

She tells me about their drive to the lake, about the noises the car made, about the clouds in the distance that never came close enough for rain. I listen, keeping my expression as clear as I can. Forcing smiles and nodding at just the right times. I listen, knowing that someday—sooner than I like—her stories will end. I listen, knowing that tears will come soon enough.

I have pondered the tears. Who are they for?

For myself? Yes, there are plenty for selfish me. I was

blessed with the most compassionate and lively mother and friend. I never appreciated all she did for me, and now, the best thing I can do for her is to sit and listen. It seems like nothing, but when she insists, "I need to tell her something," I know in my heart she needs to be heard, even if she can't find the words.

My tears pour out continually for Mama. She has lost more of her memory than she has kept. She is aware enough of what is happening to her to be terrified of tomorrow. I mourn for the vibrant woman she once was. That part of her is gone.

I've shed many more tears for my dad, knowing that he fights this disease every hour of every day. It has stolen his freedom, his partner, and his love. His battle is real and wearisome. He's tired, yet he perseveres. I pray over and over for his strength.

And then, when my tears are almost exhausted, I cry and pray for my husband. I am grateful for his devotion, but I also pray that he will have the strength for the future. Part of me fears that when this dreadful terror has finished with Mama, it may turn its wrath on me.

But all of that will come later. The tears and prayers will comingle. They will become one giant, un-sort-out-able thing. They will take my breath away and then let me breathe again.

Later.

For now, I listen.

"Do you remember when we were kids on Robin Hood Drive?"

Kim Black is a genre mixologist and an award-winning author of several novels and children's books. She is inspired by strong women, both real and fictional, and enjoys blowing things up and making readers cry.
www.kimblackink.com

THE MIRACLE

Linda Broday

Sometimes a date stuck in a man's head like stubborn horse nettle. July 22, 1952, was Levi Taggart's. Twenty years ago exactly to the day, at barely ten o'clock in the morning, his father had lifted a Colt automatic pistol to his temple and fired, the act thereby removing him from the multitude of problems on his shoulders. Levi had been fourteen.

With thoughts whirling and the past and present mirroring in his mind, an unrelenting south Texas wind whistled through the dead crop and kicked up a dust cloud around him.

He knelt amid the shriveled corn stalks on his farm, grabbed a handful of dirt, and let it sift through his fingers. Bone dry. No rain in four months had laid the ground to waste. The land, the crops, prayers, and his soul were as parched as California's Death Valley.

In the left pocket of his faded overalls was an overdue notice from the bank. The bulge in his right pocket offered permanent relief from problems.

Dirt still clinging to his fingers, his hand moved closer toward a final solution.

But what about his two children? They were the only thing that might stop him from following his father. With Nate and Sarah's mother lying dead in the grave not even three months, they'd likely go to an orphanage. Lord knew Levi's mother wouldn't take them to raise. She'd made that clear. Levi had heard about orphanages and he couldn't bear the thought of Nate and little Sarah being mistreated. The people there probably wouldn't let Sarah cling to her favorite blanket for comfort. Or see Nate at nine, fighting back tears, trying hard to be a man when he hadn't gotten to be much of a boy yet.

Levi cleared his throat and tried to settle his mind on solutions. Maybe he could sell some things. But what? His old Ford pickup had broke down. The tractor halfway ran but he couldn't farm without that. A few pieces of jewelry that had belonged to his wife wouldn't fetch enough to pay the light bill.

A small hand touched his shoulder and he jumped, not expecting the kids to follow him out here.

"Daddy, I'm hungry." Six-year-old Sarah's voice was halting, barely louder than a whisper.

Behind him, Nate spoke in an equally quiet tone. "Don't bother Daddy. I'll try to find you something, Sis."

Shame washed over Levi to have his boy trying to be the grown-up. "No, Son, that's my job." He stood and swung Sarah up in his arms, brushing the blonde hair out of her face. "Let's go see what I can scrounge up. Then maybe we'll go visit with your mama down the road under the live oak tree on the hill."

Sarah wound her arm around his neck. "Can she hear me when I talk to her?"

"Yes, I believe she can." And she likely heard him too when he cried her name at night while the kids slept. She must think him nothing but a big failure. The hard truth wiggled into his brain. Marianne had surely bore witness to his inabilities.

"I'll tell Mama about the marble I found. And the frog living under our house," Nate said.

"Just as soon as I find you something to eat."

They walked across the field and went through the kitchen door. The stillness of the house struck him as it always did when Levi came in. It, too, seemed to weep.

Levi set Sarah down. "Go play while I fix breakfast."

After she ran off, he put the gun away and opened the pantry door. The shelves were empty save for a smidgen of flour, enough coffee for one more pot, and a fourth cup of pancake mix. His chickens had stopped laying, but oddly he'd found three eggs on the back porch that morning. Where they'd come from, he didn't know. Neighbors he guessed. They sometimes shared what they had. At sight of the eggs, gratefulness had burst from his heart and he'd saved them for Nate to cook in the event he carried through with his plan.

Weevils were in the pancake mix, and Levi started to throw it out but stopped. After sifting them out, he stirred up the little bit of batter, trying not to think about tomorrow.

Or the next day.

It didn't take long to make the meal. He stood looking at the pitiful fare and called the kids. Both wore long, solemn faces as they sat at the table. Trying to ignore his rumbling stomach, he set the plates in front of them, adding glasses of water.

"We're out of butter and milk. I'm sorry. At least this is filling."

Nate glanced up at him, his gaze searching. "Where's yours, Daddy?"

"Uh, I already ate. I'll be outside working on the truck." Levi hurried out before he could ask another question and force more lies.

He made it to the pickup, opened the door, and sat in the driver's seat before he let the sobs come. A failure. Even the sorriest kind of man provided for his family. The sound of the back door slamming jarred him to life. He wouldn't let Nate and Sarah see him like this. Climbing out, he opened the hood and began tinkering with wires, hoses, and brushes. It wouldn't fix his dead battery or the broken head gasket.

Nate jostled his elbow as he tried to fit under the hood. "We finished, Daddy, and I washed the dishes."

"It was real good," Sarah added softly. "Can we visit Mama now?"

Levi raised, lowered the hood, and wiped his hands on a

rag. "We sure can, honey."

With Sarah between them, Levi and Nate took a hand and they walked to the little cemetery and stood beneath the big live oak that shaded the small plot.

"Hi, Mama." Sarah squatted in front of the marker Levi had made. "I hope you can see me. I love you very, very much."

Tears filled Nate's eyes. "We're trying, Mama, but it's hard. I wish you didn't have to go. I wish you were here. I wish everything was good again. If you can, will you tell God we need rain real bad?" He walked away, turning his back, staring into the distance.

The boy needed space and Levi gave him that. He knew the struggles of trying to make sense of a grown-up's world.

They didn't stay long and the sun was getting hot even though it was only mid-morning. Besides, he had things to get to. He told Nate to go to the next farm and play with his friend, giving him orders not to come home until supper.

A measure of disquiet flickered in Nate's brown gaze. "I'll stay here with you, Daddy. You might—" his voice broke, his chin quivering with a fear he likely didn't fully understand. "You might need me."

"No, Son." Levi laid a hand on his boy's thin shoulder. "Go play. I'll be fine. I promise. Pick your sister up at the Andrews's house before you come home."

Apprehension still filled the boy's eyes. "I will."

Levi breathed easier when Nate started toward his friend's farm. Then Levi left Sarah with her little playmate across the road.

Free to walk the six miles into town, he set off. He wouldn't come home without something for the kids to eat. He was determined to find some type of work, dig ditches if he had to. The first three places he inquired at had nothing, but the owner of a mechanic shop promised a ten-dollar bill if he could fix the timing belt on the mayor's Chevrolet by five o'clock.

Ben Dixon rubbed the back of his neck. "I don't have a minute to work on it and the mayor wants it now or he'll take it somewhere else." He sighed. "Patience has never been his strong suit and I can't afford to lose his business."

"I'll get it running," Levi promised, thinking of what ten dollars would buy in food.

By quitting time, he had the Impala purring like a kitten. Dixon handed him ten dollars. "Say, I might have a full-time job if you're interested."

Levi told him about the kids and the fact he lived outside of town. "I wouldn't be able to come in at eight. There's the kids to get settled and my pickup's broke down so I'll have to walk."

Dixon asked what it needed to get in working order and Levi told him. He went to the back and returned with a battery and the new part. "Pay me for these when you can. By the way, I'll take you home. I go out almost that far to get to my place."

Thankfulness for a caring stranger washed over Levi like a dam burst.

"I think I can get my old pickup running by morning, sir. Thank you for letting me work off the cost." Levi shook his hand. "I'll just need to stop for a few groceries before we head out if you don't mind."

Dixon laid a hand on Levi's back. "Of course not. I'm glad you came in today. I've gone through three mechanics in as many weeks, so I'd given up on finding someone for the job. I think the good Lord must've sent you."

"Maybe so. I was down to my last bit of strength and didn't know how I'd go on another day." Levi didn't mention what he'd almost done. Thank God he hadn't pulled that trigger.

A short while later with a sack of groceries, the car battery, and gasket in the back seat, Ben Dixon drove Levi home. During the drive he told his new boss about his wife's death and how hard it had been with no rain and dead crops. He found it easier to talk to Ben than it had to his own mother.

Ben pulled up in front of the house. "Taggart, we all go through hard times. There's not a man who doesn't. Help is near if we just try harder to find it."

Levi nodded. "I'll see you in the morning—eight sharp. And

thanks again."

He flew into the house, made supper, and had it ready by the time Nate came in the door with Sarah. He'd stopped and picked her up on the way. Both were astounded at all the food and for once they all got their fill.

While Nate and Sarah washed dishes, Levi went to work on the pickup. He rigged up lighting so he could work on it in the dark. One short pause to put the kids to bed then back to the job. He kept at it until he finished. After a quick bath, he slept for a couple of hours.

His heart was light, his soul at peace for the first time since Marianne died. There were lots of good people in the world ready to lend a hand. But first, a man had to set aside his pride. Miracles were alive and well for those seeking one. It called for being willing to do whatever it took to make his situation better.

Then if you were brave enough, sometimes you had to make your own miracle.

The next morning, he woke to the beautiful sound of rain pattering on the tin roof and he smiled.

Linda Broday is a New York Times and USA Today best-selling author of 28 novels and novellas. She's been a member of Texas High Plains Writers for almost twenty years. A proud moment came in 2018 when she was named WRITER OF THE YEAR by the organization. Linda loves writing about the cowboy way of life and finds plenty of inspiration at home in the Panhandle. Visit her webpage at LindaBroday.com
Amazon Author Page: amazon.com/Linda-Broday/e/B001JRXWB2
Facebook: facebook.com/lindabrodayauthor
Twitter: twitter.com/LBroday
Instagram: instagram.com/linda.broday/

A FLICKER IN AUGUST

Mary Cooke

Shelly pulled her chair closer so she could hear.

"I'm sorry if what I'm getting ready to tell you sounds negative. Not many men in their seventies pull through a heart attack the way you did. If you want to live through the next one, though, you have to restrict your activities."

Who ever told Rayford to slow down?

"Doctor, can I chop wood?"

The doctor leaned back and chuckled. "Chop wood? It's August."

Rayford's dark blue eyes flashed from the doctor to Shelly and back to the doctor. His voice sounded soft and gravelly. "You know what I'm talking about."

"Oh, I get it." Doc shook his head. "Absolutely not. The excitement could cause your heart to go out of rhythm."

After fifty-one years of marriage, Shelly and Rayford still got excited.

Rayford bit his lip.

"No plowing with your tractor. Don't lift the gas can. No coffee." He handed a list to Shelly. "Avoid these foods. They're loaded with cholesterol."

Rayford stood to go. "Much obliged."

"Thanks, Dr. Prudhomme." Shelly followed.

The doctor rushed to open the door for them. "I wish you the best."

She drove. "We'll stop by the drugstore."

Rayford folded his fists in his lap. "That ain't no way for a man to live."

The afternoon passed in silence. Shelly rushed around doing the chores. She fed the chickens and the dog. "What do you want for supper?"

"Don't we have some leftover cornbread?"

"Yep." She turned the radio on. "Let's listen to some music."

They crumbled cornbread into tumblers and poured buttermilk over it.

At sunset they turned off the radio and went to bed.

Before daylight Rayford tugged on Shelly's leg. "You won't turn me down, will you, Sweetheart?"

Wouldn't turning away and rejecting Rayford hurt him more than making love?

Afterward, she must have dozed. She patted his side of the bed to find it empty. The air smelled of coffee laced with chicory. She slid her feet into her bedroom slippers and threw on her summer housedress.

Rayford opened the squeaky door of the oven to remove a pan of fluffy golden biscuits. Sausage sizzled in the skillet. Eggs waited in a nearby bowl. "Get us some ice water. We'll go sit on the picnic table and watch the sunrise while we eat."

Shelly pitched in to help. Blackberry jam, blackstrap molasses, butter, and canned milk. Silverware and napkins. She loaded biscuits onto a plate.

Rayford followed her with two plates of fried eggs and sausage. "I'll go back for the coffee."

"I've got your milk out here."

He brought her a cup of hot water and the little jar of instant decaf. His coffee was the dark kind full of grounds and chicory.

After breakfast and the chores, he said, "Go on into town and pick up a few supplies. We're out of fresh milk. Get some day-old bread for the pup."

"I don't have to, do I?"

"You could make do, but it would be better if you'd pick up a little grub."

In town, she ran into her niece, and they visited a few minutes. "Got to get on back home and check on Rayford."

As she drove into the long driveway, she glanced at the big garden plot on the southeast side of the yard.

Plowed. They'd planned to plow it up for a fall garden. Did Jack, their son-in-law, come by while she was gone?

The International Harvester™ tractor sat by the garden gate. And the gas can. Did the tractor run out of gas? She parked her car in the shade, rolled down the windows, and removed her bag of groceries, purse on her arm.

Outside the kitchen door, the little old wagon, once red, waited with a large watermelon loaded into it. She hoped Jack took one home with him, but why didn't he put the tractor back in the shed? The carburetor must have been acting up again.

Where was Rayford?

She took the bag of groceries inside. Another fresh pot of coffee sat on the stove, and the canned milk needed to be put in the Frigidaire™. She glanced through the kitchen door into the living room. Rayford sat with his back toward her.

"Rayford," she called. "Did Jack come by? I hope you didn't get too hot." As she talked, she returned the canned milk to the fridge, along with the cold food from her bag.

He must have been taking a nap. He got up early.

She tiptoed into the living room. Rayford sat slumped and holding his cup. His face glowed with a contented smile. He was still warm.

Mary Cooke, who writes as Mary Lou Cheatham, grew up on a hill farm on the county line south of Taylorsville, Mississippi, and north of Hot Coffee. Her folks, the Greggs, sat around the fireplace on winter nights with pecans to roast and crack, while they competed to see who could tell the most intriguing stories. On summer evenings, they sat on the front porch, where they shelled peas and beans and listened to the bobcats.

Now she lives in Ransom Canyon, where she and her husband John enjoy living near her daughter and son-in-law. In the evening, they dodge skunks in their yard, watch for deer when they drive, and occasionally see a coyote.

She has had careers as a high school teacher and registered nurse. These days she is compelled to write historical novels.

FINN

Cheryle Cooper

Giselle stood frozen, peering out of mother's bay window. Between the accumulated dust on the glass and her reservoir of tears, everything looked hazy. When she felt the softness of her mother's touch, pressing into the small of her back, her cinnamon-brown face became awash in tears. "We've already picked out his name," she mumbled, referring to the tiny life growing inside of her. Then, as she gently massaged her protruding belly, she added, "There's no way I'm going to let them end his life, Mama."

At that moment, she turned and collapsed into her mother's arms, sobbing so uncontrollably that her mother began bawling, as well. Together they stumbled backward onto the couch, all the while clutching each other with tortured desperation.

"Child," her mother begged. "Calm down. Tell me what happened."

It took Giselle a few minutes to steady herself as she dabbed her eyes and nose with a matted tissue. Then, she inhaled deeply and exhaled slowly. "Well," she started. "For weeks, they told us everything was fine with the baby. In fact, when we went for the sonogram we weren't even trying to find out if we were having a boy or a girl. But... it was very clear on the monitor that we were having a boy."

She stopped and smiled ever so slightly. In return, her mother flashed a sheepish grin. "Anyway," Giselle continued, "the only thing Dr. Prokov was concerned about was my weight. He told me I wasn't gaining enough, so he gave me these supplements that were supposed to help increase my appetite."

She paused to collect her thoughts and then explained, "He said they were perfectly safe for expectant moms, that they were fennel-based to improve my digestion and eating. I even looked up the ingredients, myself, to be sure." Once more, she returned to the window. The world outside seemed miles away —so distant from the nightmare she was experiencing.

"But, weren't those the ones you said made you sick?" her mother asked.

"More than sick!" Giselle emphasized. "Violently ill. Remember?"

Nodding, her mother replied, "Yes, I do."

Again, the tears flowed. "I never took another one after that." Her voice cracked as she said, "Next thing we knew, at my follow-up appointment, they were telling us something was terribly wrong with Finn."

"Oh sweetheart," her mother groaned.

"Suddenly, they were urging us to terminate the pregnancy!" she cried. "I mean, can you believe it?"

Her mother rocked back and forth on the sofa, shaking her head and wiping away tears. Finally, she asked, "Do you think maybe stopping the medication had something to do with them finding something wrong with the baby?"

"No, Mama," Giselle said, resolute, with folded arms. "I honestly don't think so. Plus, I never told the doctor that I had stopped taking them."

"You didn't? Why not?

"Because I didn't want him to force me to keep taking them," she said. "Especially after getting so sick that first time."

Her mother sighed. "Oh my."

"Anyway, Sam and I were, and are, devastated," she declared. "On that day, there was Dr. Prokov and the hospital's risk manager pressuring us to end this pregnancy, 'for the good of the baby,' they kept saying. But, they never told us exactly what was wrong—only that the baby showed signs of insurmountable birth defects, they said."

Springing to her feet, her mother joined her at the window and held her close. "Baby girl," she reassured. "It's going to be alright. You and Sam, by God's grace, are going to get through this."

But, Giselle pulled away sharply. "That's just the thing, Mama!" she stammered. "I don't know where Sam really stands anymore. I mean, at first we couldn't stop crying and clinging to each other." She hesitated, feeling overpowered by anger and sadness. "But, then, he started getting real quiet. I couldn't tell if maybe he was siding with Dr. Prokov. He kept saying he needed time to think through things and to pray. What is there to think through? There shouldn't be a question in the world that we're going to have this baby—no matter what."

"Well... now, honey," her mother interrupted. "Sam will do the right thing. I just know it. You can't assume the worse until you guys have had some real time to sort this out. When does he get back from Copenhagen?"

"Copenhagen was last week, Mom," Giselle huffed. "He flies home from Chicago tomorrow night. Meanwhile, the risk manager has been bugging me every other day, saying I've got to come in now for a consultation. A consultation! Is that the new name for preparations to kill a child?"

Her mother squeezed her arms. "Daughter, have you sought the Lord?" she asked.

Staring downward at her mother's well-worn carpeting, Giselle ceased stirring, knowing in her heart she had done more fretting than praying. "No," she confessed, feeling the instant sting of conviction.

Tenderly, her mother recited John 14:27: "Peace I leave with you, My peace I give unto you: not as the world giveth, give I unto you. Let not your heart be troubled, neither let it be afraid." Then, they embraced.

"Thank you, Mama," she gushed, resting her head on her mother's frail shoulders.

"I love you," her mother whispered. "Just give it to God, baby girl, and you can't go wrong. Give it to God."

Giselle's husband, Sam, was a project engineer. He worked for a multinational cement and industrial minerals corporation that had factories scattered around the globe. One day he could be in Hong Kong; the next day the south of France; the day after that Phoenix, Arizona—all in one month. Sitting at their kitchen counter sipping warm tea, Giselle waited anxiously for him to arrive.

It was a little after seven when she heard the garage door open; and, not long afterward, Sam came striding in through the laundry room door.

For sure, he looked bedraggled from traveling, but striking just the same. In fact, his piercing gray eyes and rugged features never failed to melt her heart. "Hello," she greeted him, suddenly feeling the nerves creep up her spine and settle predominately around her neck.

He dropped his luggage on the floor by the bookcase and approached her with a kiss. "Hi, Babe." They hugged for the longest.

His muscular arms gave her the consolation she craved. "How was your trip?" she asked, attempting to break the ice.

He flopped down on their brand new settee. With his hand, he combed back-and-forth through his jet black hair. Giselle knew that sign very well. Something was bothering him—big time.

Visibly winded, he finally said, "Man, do I have a lot to tell you."

She stiffened. Her curiosity piqued. "Really?"

They stared at each other for a moment before he spoke low and methodically. "First of all, I wasn't in Chicago on business," he disclosed.

"No?"

"No," he said, shaking his head. "I went there to see Arnie."

"Arnie?" Giselle repeated. "Isn't he that friend of yours who runs the chemical lab?"

Her husband nodded. "Yep!"

"But why?" she asked, bewildered.

He stood and began to pace. "I've got to start from the beginning," Sam said. "From my trip to Copenhagen."

"Copenhagen?" she whispered, her gaze firmly fixed on him.

Again, he raked through his hair with his hand, appearing to grabble internally. Finally, he blurted out, "The day they told us something was wrong with Finn was one of the worse days of my life."

Caressing her tummy, Giselle concurred, "Yes. I know. Me, too."

"Well, if you'll recall, I still had to get on that plane a few days later even though I felt like dying instead. But I had no choice. The company needed me."

"Yes," she said. "I know."

"Well," he elaborated, "I never told you this, but my flight was delayed for at least three hours. It was a mess. But it was enough time for me to run into an old co-worker, Ben Trussle. Ben was sitting in the next gate over, scheduled to fly out to Florida. His flight was delayed, too."

"Ben Trussle?"

"Yes," Sam said. "He worked in our compliance division. I hardly ever ran into him. But since we both had the time that day, we got to talking. That's when he told me he landed a much higher paying job with another company."

"Okay," Giselle said, asking herself, where is he going with all of this?

"He said he needed more pay to cover attorney's fees for a lawsuit he was freshly embroiled in."

"Sam," she coaxed. "What has this got to do with anything?"

"Giselle!" her husband interjected. "Ben Trussle and his

wife are suing the same medical practice that Prokov is with—for fraud and malpractice."

"What!" She gasped. "Are you serious? They're suing Dr. Prokov?"

"No, not Prokov," he corrected. "Ben's wife's doctor is a man named Jerry Southam. He is in the same OB-GYN group as Prokov, and they are suing him."

"Oh my! Why? What happened?"

"Apparently, when his wife was only ten-weeks pregnant, she was injected with what was supposed to be a safe allergy shot. But later, they discovered there was some kind of horrific mix-up. What they gave her was linked to severe birth defects."

Covering her mouth, Giselle screamed, "Oh no!"

"But, instead of telling her and Ben the truth, they coerced them into terminating the pregnancy to cover up for their ghastly mistake," he revealed. "They told them their baby had major problems and that it would be much better to terminate."

"Did they go through with it?" she inquired.

Tilting his head, he confirmed, "Tragically, they did." He added, "They couldn't handle the pressure. It's a whole long story about how exactly they discovered the fatal error; and all the twists and turns. But, nevertheless, it got me wondering if maybe Prokov, too, had blundered with us."

Shocked, she had no words.

"Things just weren't adding up," Sam said. "So once I returned home from Denmark, I called Arnie right away to see if he could do a chemical analysis on those supplements. The ones Prokov gave you."

Holding back tears, she asked him, "Is that why you've been so distant with me all of this time?"

"Sweetheart, I didn't want to alarm you until I had my final proof," he admitted. "I mean if a doctor in the same group made such a terrible mistake that cost a child his life, I had to find out if the same thing had happened to us."

"It's a good thing I didn't throw those awful pills out," Giselle reasoned. "'Tho' I wanted to."

"I'm glad you didn't either," her husband said. "When I saw them in the cabinet, I took a few with me and headed out to Arnie's lab."

"Wow!" My man is such a hero, she mused.

"Anyway, after he tested them for me," Sam went on, "Arnie said they were not benign appetite boosters at all. Instead, Prokov gave you an Amethopterin-type drug which is an immunosuppressive agent and highly toxic."

"Oh dear Lord!" she shrieked.

"Worse still, that drug can cause serious birth defects to an unborn child," he declared, rushing to her side. They held each other so tight, she could hardly breathe.

"I only took one," Giselle stated. "Do you think one could harm the baby?"

"I have no idea," he said. "But it's obvious, to me, that when they realized their mistake, they panicked and wanted a way to cover their tracks."

"Yes," she added, "especially with another family suing one of their own doctors for a similar error. Wow, how evil!"

He motioned in agreement. "It is."

Giselle looked Sam square in his eyes. "But we're not going to murder our own child, you hear me? I don't care how much they hound us," she proclaimed. "Maybe one pill didn't do serious damage. After all, I was much further along when this happened than Ben's wife was. And our baby was more developed than theirs. There's always that hope. We've got to stand our ground and keep praying for our precious Finn."

He kissed her forehead lightly and whispered, "Of course, Babe. I wouldn't have it any other way." Then, he said, "Besides, Dr. Prokov and that whole medical team have to be held accountable for this. Lives are at stake."

Giselle laid her head on his chest and closed her eyes. "Praise God," she crooned, feeling enveloped in a renewed peace. "Praise God."

Cheryle Cooper lives in Amarillo, Texas, where she owns and operates Expert Editing – a home-based writing, editing, and private tutoring business. Over the years, Cheryle has had numerous articles and stories published in regional magazines. Her interests include theology, nutrition, physical fitness, music, supporting homeschooling, and defending civil liberties and basic freedoms, to name a few. She is currently working on her first children's book along with writing other inspirational short-stories and nonfiction articles that endeavor to give glory and honor to God.

IMPOSSIBLE DREAMS

Dahna Danli

A cold breeze whipped through the second floor of the abandoned office building, stirring up old flyers scattered across the concrete. Torn sheets of heavy plastic rustled like forgotten ghosts. Sarah shivered, huddled deeper into her hoodie, and watched drops of rain splash through grimy, broken window panes. She breathed deeply, trying to find that fresh rain scent, but it was tainted by the stink of garbage from the alley below.

She sighed.

She used to love the rain. That was before she was homeless. Before her parents died and the courts moved her to L.A. to live with her only living relatives, an alcoholic aunt and her three kids. Sarah wondered if the woman had sobered up long enough even to realize she was gone. Doubtful. As long as Anita got the monthly trust fund allowance, she wouldn't care.

"You gonna sit over there and freeze?" Travis called.

Sarah's eyes cut over to glare at him. He and the five other members of their tribe were in a middle room gathered around a dented metal firepit someone threw away. Wood crackled, offering warmth. She turned her head away.

"Suit yourself," he huffed.

She scooted out of view to lean against one of the thick

concrete support pillars and looked at the gray sky beyond the dilapidated neighboring building. The wet winter weather matched her mood.

Last night had been bad. Really bad. She never dreamed Travis would get so desperate for a fix that he would offer to let his drug dealer use her as payment. *Jerk.* When he asked her to run away with him during Summer break, it seemed like the answer to her prayers. Not so much now.

"Hey, Falcon?"

Sarah looked around at the blonde girl with big blue eyes that had influenced her 'tribe' name. "Hi, Rabbit."

The girl held out a nutrition bar. "I had an extra. You want it?"

Sarah smiled. "Thanks, but you keep it. I think I'll wrap up in some of this plastic and go to the community center."

"No one needs to be goin' anywhere," Travis declared.

Sarah looked past Rabbit to see Travis standing in the doorway with Eagle, the self-proclaimed leader of their little band of not-so-merry people.

"Why do you care where I go?" Sarah challenged.

"She just wants to go see that old man," Travis grumbled, resentment evident in his tone. "They sit and talk—for hours."

Sarah sneered. Mr. Yoshi, the "old man," had noticed her martial arts skills while teaching self-defense classes at the community center and started talking to her after class. She treasured those conversations and wanted his advice now. "I can bring back food which should make everyone happy."

Eagle turned narrowed eyes on Travis. "I don't care what they do if it brings us food. No one else wants to go out in this rain."

Travis stared at Eagle for a minute, then backed down. Instead, he motioned as if shooing away a fly. "Go on. Go see the old man. Let him fill your head with impossible dreams."

"Glad to," Sarah answered defiantly, standing. She tore off a sheet of plastic, wrapped it over her head and shoulders, and left.

By the time she reached the center, she was almost soaked through. The director, Gail, was there and brought Sarah a couple of towels as she dripped water just inside the door. "If you get a mop, I'll clean that up," Sarah offered.

"Don't worry. It's been so quiet today it would be nice to have something to do. What are you doing out in this weather? You could get sick."

Sarah shrugged, finding it difficult to make eye contact. She hated having to beg. "My friends are hungry. I thought maybe I could get some of those nutrition bars for them. And I hoped Mr. Yoshi was here. I'd like to talk to him."

"Of course, dear." Gail turned to one of the assistants. "Jessica, would you please let Mr. Yoshi know Falcon is here." The girl nodded, and Gail turned back to Sarah, lowering her voice. "You know we're not supposed to give food for more than one person, but I think we can make an exception today. I doubt we'll have many visitors. Remind me how many of you there are."

"Seven, including me."

Gail nodded. "Ok. I'll be right back." She looked toward a doorway in the back. "There's Mr. Yoshi now." She smiled and headed for one of the back rooms, passing Mr. Yoshi with a nod of her head.

The old man nodded back, then smiled warmly at Sarah as he approached. "I didn't think we'd see you today."

"My friends were hungry, but I also wanted to talk to you."

He studied her for a moment, his expression becoming concerned, then indicated the unoccupied sitting area.

She took a seat on one of the chairs, and he sat beside her.

"What's troubling you, *magomusume*?"

Sarah smiled at the Japanese term. She barely remembered her biological grandparents, so to have Mr. Yoshi call her granddaughter gave her a warm feeling. Before she could say anything, Gail came back with a plastic bag and handed it to Sarah.

"I put enough in there for each of you to have a nutrition bar, an apple, and peanut butter."

"Oh, Gail. Thank you, but I didn't expect you to be so generous."

"As I said, it's a slow day. And someone needs to eat those apples before they go bad." She gave Sarah a wink and went to the desk.

Mr. Yoshi chuckled. "You have friends here, Sarah," he told her, keeping his voice low so the others wouldn't hear her real name. "You've earned it. The help you voluntarily give here is appreciated."

"I like it here. I like to help. And it makes me feel less like a freeloader."

Mr. Yoshi shook his head. "None of us see you that way, but I know your situation troubles you." He held up a finger before Sarah could respond and looked over to the desk. "Gail, would you mind if I took some time away to speak to our young friend elsewhere?"

"Not at all."

Sarah noticed the knowing smile Gail gave him and wondered what that was about.

"I doubt this day is going to get better," Gail continued. "Rain is predicted for two more days." Sarah groaned, and Gail laughed. "I agree."

Mr. Yoshi leaned close. "Come, child. Let's get a hot meal in that stomach of yours." Sarah opened her mouth to protest, but he cut her off. "Don't argue. It's disrespectful to your elders." He winked, and Sarah grinned, something she hadn't done much over the past two years.

Mr. Yoshi grabbed two umbrellas from the stand, then held the door open for her.

The rain had eased to a drizzle, but the clouds remained dark blue and heavy, threatening more to come. Here, Sarah could smell the fresh rain and took deep cleansing breaths as they splashed along the sidewalk to a small diner in the next block.

After they ordered, Mr. Yoshi gazed at her, waiting for her to speak.

She hesitated but finally told him about Travis and the night before. "I thought he cared, but that proved all he cares about is himself."

"What did you do?"

"Hurt the dealer where it counts and left Travis to get high."

"I'm glad you know how to defend yourself, but I worry. Living on the streets is dangerous. And I know you aren't happy."

"No, I'm not. I only ran away five months ago, but it feels like years. I don't fit in well with the others, but because of my skills from the martial arts and gymnastics classes I've taken, I'm good at Parkour and free-running. Makes me useful."

"I'm familiar with Parkour."

"Free-running is Parkour with gymnastics. A lot like what Jackie Chan did in his movies. That's why the tribe always wants me to steal for us. I only agree when it's for food, but I don't like breaking the law just to eat."

"Can you say no?"

Sarah frowned. "I could, but they might disown me. There's safety in numbers." She fought back tears. "My parents would be so disappointed. They raised me to be a good person but look at me."

"Your circumstances are not your fault."

"Yes, they are. I agreed to run away with Travis. I put myself in this position."

"I can't argue with that, but the arrangement with your aunt was not good either. Living in a two-bedroom apartment with four other people, her children bullying you and her boyfriend being inappropriate to you. That is unacceptable."

"I started to report her, but where else would I go? And who would believe a sixteen-year-old kid?" Sarah hung her head. "Maybe I should have stayed. All I've done is trade one bad situation for another."

Their meals were delivered, and they talked as they ate. "I hope this doesn't upset you," Mr. Yoshi said, "but after what happened to you last night, I don't want to wait."

Sarah looked at him, suddenly wary. "What?"

"I checked, and you were right. You haven't been reported as a runaway. I assume you stayed in school so you wouldn't be truant since you keep your books and papers at the center? Is that correct?"

Sarah nodded. "You said that was important, but Travis makes it hard. He thinks it's stupid for me to keep going."

"I won't tell you my opinion of what Travis thinks. What I will say is that I spoke to a lawyer two weeks ago."

Sarah's eyes grew big, and her mouth dropped open. "Lawyer?"

Mr. Yoshi quickly continued. "The young man I became a guardian for, Michael, has moved away to attend college. I need someone else to help around my house and his room is now vacant. Compensation is room and board and a small allowance. Because you only have a year and a half until you turn eighteen, the lawyer said it would be better if your aunt signed a notarized Caregiver Authorization Affidavit to allow you to live with me legally. We would not need to involve slow courts, and I would not be arrested for harboring a runaway. That would give me authority for your school and basic medical needs."

Sarah's eyes widened further. "You would do that for me?"

"You know I think of you as a granddaughter. When Michael moved, I thought of you. I did not become a volunteer with the center simply to teach self-defense. I hoped to make a difference where needed, and you are in need. I wish to help you."

Sarah felt a glimmer of hope dance across her heart. "That would be great. But do you think my aunt will sign? She likes getting that money from my trust, supposedly for my care."

Mr. Yoshi smiled. "I can think of two points that might convince her. One, if you agree, is that she can keep getting the money until you turn eighteen and take over the trust. I don't need it. Two, it would be in her favor to sign the document to avoid an investigation. Her failure to report you as a runaway could be against her as well as her lifestyle. I will not hesitate to mention these points." He leaned a little closer over the table. "I can be very convincing."

Sarah grinned. "I would appreciate your help very much."

"Good. Then it's settled. Tomorrow I will print the form, speak to your aunt, and drive her to the notary myself. No point in waiting."

"I don't know how to thank you."

"Simple. Stay in school. Make good grades. Work hard. Do something good with your life."

Sarah nodded. "I will."

"I believe you. Otherwise, I wouldn't offer. But you should understand I have rules. Things like no drinking or drugs, no skipping school, do your chores, be respectful, and so on. Do you think you can do that?"

"Gladly. Those are basically the same rules my parents had."

"I suspected as much," he said with a smile. "After we're finished here, would you like to see the room Michael had? It's on the other side of the house from mine so you will have privacy and comes with a bathroom of your own. You could bring your books and school work if you need to get more done before tomorrow's classes, but you don't have to stay if you aren't yet comfortable."

"No, I would like that. But can we deliver the food Gail gave me to the others and let me say goodbye?"

"Of course."

Mr. Yoshi paid the bill, and they walked back to the center. When they entered, Gail looked up, searching their faces.

"She agreed," Mr. Yoshi announced.

Gail grinned and came rushing over to hug Sarah, tears forming in her eyes. "I'm so glad."

"You knew?"

"Yes. He discussed it with me. He has helped three other clients from here, but he doesn't accept just anyone. We all agreed you would be a good choice."

"Thank you," Sarah breathed.

"We're going to get her school things, drop off the food, and let her say goodbye. Then I'm going to show her the room," Mr. Yoshi said.

"More like a suite," Gail commented. "I helped set it up a few years ago when he told me what he wanted to do. In addition to the bedroom and bathroom, there's a small sitting area with a comfy stuffed chair and ottoman, a desk, and a mini-fridge and microwave. Great for studying."

"I didn't want to be disturbed by a student's hunger for a midnight snack," Mr. Yoshi laughed. "I need my sleep."

Sarah's eyes darted between them. "Really?"

They nodded.

"Get your things," Mr. Yoshi urged.

Sarah ran to the lockers and grabbed her school supplies, then Mr. Yoshi drove to the abandoned building. He followed her inside, waiting nearby to help in case of trouble.

"Took you long enough," Tavis accused when she walked in.

She handed the food to Rabbit and walked up to him. "I'm tired of you talking to me like that and offering to let your dealer use me in trade for drugs. I'm done."

"What?" He clenched a fist.

"Try it," Sarah dared.

He stared at her.

She didn't break eye contact. "You can't win," she warned.

He grabbed her wrist and yanked, but she was ready. She broke his grip and spun around with a low kick, sweeping him off his feet.

He landed hard, grunting, and glared, his face turning red.

"Don't ever touch me again."

The others watched but didn't move.

"You want more?"

"Not worth it," he mumbled, sullen.

"No, you're not. You were a colossal mistake. I'm out of here. I have "impossible dreams" to follow. Take care, Rabbit. Good luck all."

Mr. Yoshi smiled, nodding with approval. "Well done. Let's go home.

Dahna Danli is a Sci-fi and Fantasy writer, adventurer, and friend to cats. The above story gives the reader a glimpse into the history of the main character in the upcoming release, tentatively titled *Sarah Among the Stars, Book One: Lost and Found.*

THE MOWER INCIDENT

Bobbette Doerrie

N ew worlds aren't found only by intrepid explorers. Even when the challenges are not on the same level, a person entering a new, unknown world is still exploring and taking risks.

When my new husband brought me, a city girl, to the farm, he pointed to the big green John Deere tractor and said, "That's MY tractor," and pointed to the riding lawn mower and said, "That's YOUR tractor."

Later, I learned that not all wives climb on tractors or help out as mechanic's helpers, but I agreed that "pulling together" was a mantra I could agree with. I found out later this term replied to plow horses, and sometimes I felt like one because the intensity of the work was very different from my chores in town. There were compensations, though. There is great satisfaction in the scent of a newly plowed field or wheat I planted, singing softly as the wind played in the golden heads.

I learned that electricity is not reliable, and ice storms, high wind, and lightning strikes can take it away in an instant. Water can be lost for days because the well depends on electricity. Our access depended on courageous line workers from the electric cooperative, climbing in the bitter cold or howling winds to repair the lines or downed power poles. Machinery breaks down; it is just a matter of time, and it was my fault only if I didn't check the oil, listen for odd sounds or feel unusual vibrations. A poorly parked grain truck can sink into hidden mud when it is loaded with freshly harvested wheat; a combine can pull it out, but only if there are enough chains. The driver has to get the chains, they are staggeringly heavy, and the driver will go back for more chains if there aren't enough.

I knew the concept of "neighboring" to help others who needed a hand. It took on new meaning on the farm because it became the way people in the country survive when there is a fire, Death comes to call, and the crops have to be harvested, or a very ignorant new wife arrives and doesn't know how to mix weed spray or to fill the bathtub before a blizzard for water. The coffee shop is a very important place because it is where farmers trade tales, drink coffee, and solve the problems of the political world. Funny stories travel at the speed of mouth. John Ray, our neighbor, was one of the most popular storytellers.

I loved mowing with "my tractor." Unlike teaching, my paid job, with mowing you can tell if you have made progress immediately, just by looking. But mowing is "a farm job," and like most farm jobs, it takes longer than you think it will, usually has other jobs you have to do first, and involves breakdowns or unexpected crises.

On a farm, weeds are a problem, especially around equipment in the yard. My nemesis was the grain auger, a thirty-foot long tube with a solid corkscrew inside and a pipe frame with three tires on it, used to transfer grain into the big silver storage bins. Weeds grow under it if you don't mow or spray them, and they have to be eliminated. As a new farm woman, I looked at those weeds as a challenge, and I was determined to conquer them. There was a part of the frame about chest high in the middle, but the mower could fit under it, even if the rider couldn't. Leaning back, I could sneak up slowly under the frame, mow to the middle, controlling the motion with my foot on the brake, then shift direction and back off to reposition and mow the next section. My farmer husband was annoyed by the safety mechanism that turns off the engine if there is no rider in the seat and bypassed it long before I arrived; there are rules against that for a reason.

Late one summer, I slowly mowed under the auger frame, my foot on the brake, feeling totally in charge and proud of myself. Unfortunately, as I leaned back to get a little farther, my foot slipped off the brake. Away the mower sped, wiping me off the seat on the rough pipes and landing on my back, my shirt and bra in rags. I didn't have time to recover because the mower, blades flying, sped off toward the grain bin, hit a low place in the farmyard, and took a left turn, heading directly for the combine across the yard. It was nearly harvest, and we didn't have time to fix it if it was damaged. I ran like harvest depended on my catching it, rags flying, trying to catch it before the collision, and I managed to jump into the seat and halt it just before the wreck.

Panting, for the first time, I thought about what I had done. I had missed the sharp flying blades, and something else, too: our neighbor John Ray, who was stopped in his pickup, watching, with a giant grin on his face.

Bobette Doerrie spent her "first life" in a town, chasing four children and teaching junior high and high school as a banker's wife, part of an active church, and writing poetry. Her "second life" began when a friend from college arrived on her doorstep and found her with most children in college and a single mother. What Jerome didn't tell her was he had a crush on her in their McMurry days, which explained why his eyes twinkled as she explained she was single now and still teaching. Before a year was out, they were married, and she was learning the complexities of farm life and still teaching for "off-farm income," which turned out to be a common activity for farm wives. The children are all grown now, and between them, there are six children and twelve grandchildren. Both are retired, Bobette after forty-one years of teaching, and Jerome after several years of teaching and fifty years of farming. They are active as officers in Silver-Haired Legislature, astronomy outreach, emergency management communications, and in other service-minded organizations. Bobette writes memoirs, poetry, and teaching articles.

BLOOD & HONEY

Hunter Fithen

Taste of blood. An excited drum beat in his head. Ache of muscles in his neck. The blurry bar crowd swirls around him. The punch to the face and the drink in him prompt a response.

Rage.

The boy whirls around, fist connecting with the man's mouth, mashing against skin and lips, yellow teeth slicing his knuckles open.

The man staggers back and spits.

Curses are exchanged.

A crowd surrounds them howling and cheering. The empty spaces of the bar are filled with smoke and neon and lust and greed.

The man said Redskins ain't so tough. He'll see. The boy ducks beneath the juggernaut's swing and gut-punches. The man vomits from the hit. The boy drives him into the floor and pounds his head into the battered old boards until the audience pulls him off.

The crowd roars and curses and drinks. Blood runs from the boy's mouth down through the sweat on his chest. He stands over his enemy, eyes fixed on the man's belt. He had a knife the whole time.

Uncle Mato comes out of the crowd and raises the boy's fist into the air, declaring him champion of the bar. Again. The crowd can't get enough.

Mato leads him out of the human arena, and they sit. He grabs a bottle of whiskey and makes the boy swish the bitten tongue in his mouth and spit the liquid hellfire onto the old boards and tells him he's done good. Says this is why nobody crosses the Chieftains.

The boy doesn't care.

All he wants to do is fight. Just like he does every night. Drink, fight, smoke, chew, spit and fight some more.

All night. Every night.

He sleeps during the day and treats his knuckles with ice and bandages. It's how he's made his living since he was fifteen. That's when his Uncle Mato got out of prison. Now he's 21 and angry as ever.

Angry at his father for being an abusive drunk.

Angry at mom for letting it happen.

Angry at the Tribal Police for not stopping it.

Angry at his own gang – the Apache Chieftains – for saving him from one hell, only to lead him into another.

Uncle Mato joined in prison. Became a high-ranking member by the time he was released. Now he ran security for the Indian casino out in Saddleback County. The whole operation was a front, and Mato's job was to keep the real business on the down-low. And he was damn good at that.

There was only one thing in the world the boy wasn't angry at:

Cady Collins.

A pretty white girl who'd knocked at his trailer door one morning a few years ago. She gave him cookies and asked if he had time to let her talk about Jesus. He told her hell no and slammed the door in her face like he had to a dozen others before.

But then she'd knocked again. Annoyed, but surprised, he'd answered again, and she'd told him that what he'd just done was extremely rude, but she forgave him for being an asshole and wanted him to have a nice day. Then she'd left.

They'd gone to school together. She was beautiful and popular and had no need for rejects like him in her perfect little life. But the day after the incident at his trailer, she had come over to his lunch table and apologized to him for what she said.

Another social outcast like himself sitting nearby started laughing at Cady. The boy pegged him in the face with an apple, and they both got detention. But even after that, Cady would still talk to him. She was the only person who ever did. Cady Collins was the only friend he ever had in the world. And no matter what he did, Cady would always stop by to check on him.

She didn't condone his choices. Not at all. But he liked that she didn't pull any punches. She didn't preach to him, but she definitely spoke her mind. She was his only point of reference to keep from going crazy.

He thought about Cady as he sat at the bar and drank whiskey and fought three more men throughout the course of the night.

Daybreak came and the bar emptied and everyone inside eventually stumbled out into the world again. The boy sat at the bar, sobering up with a glass of tap water while Uncle Mato counted his money from the fights.

"You really handed 'em their asses tonight, kid." The boy didn't say anything. "You keep that up, and you'll be a true Chieftain soon."

The boy spoke, "I don't know if I can do it."

Mato froze. Eyes blazed from his tattooed face, cigar nearly falling out of his mouth. "What the hell did you just say, boy?"

"I said I don't know if I can be a true Chieftain."

"You're saying you can kick that much ass, be that freaking ruthless, but you can't stomach taking a scalp?"

The boy took another sip of water. The knowledge that scalping was part of the Chieftains initiation process made his headache that much worse as he imagined a blade scraping across the top of his skull.

Mato smacked the water out of his hand. The glass spilled and shattered all over the bloody floor. "Tell me another joke, boy." He didn't respond. "This gang is your family. And your family is waiting on you to become a man." The boy just stared at the shelves full of liquor. His uncle Mato grabbed him by his sore and bloody mouth and forced it open, clamping the sides. "You freaking hear me?"

He seared with pain and rage inside. Everything in him screamed to take Mato to the ground and beat him until he foamed at the mouth.

But Mato's men were with him, as usual. No more than ten feet away. And if he laid a finger on Mato, they would beat him till he could never walk or eat normally again.

"I said, do you freaking hear me?"

He shook his head yes. He did it slowly, to show Mato he could take the pain. That his grip wasn't so tough. Mato saw the fire in the boy's eyes and let go. "Then get your shit together," he shoved his stacks of money into his jacket and barked at his men to get the car ready. "You're a warrior, boy. That's all you are. You fight for this family. That's all you do. That's all you will ever do. Don't challenge your destiny."

The boy waited at the bar for Mato to walk out and the rumble of the engine to fade away into the distance. Then he was alone.

He left and walked northbound on County Road 5, past the wheat fields, the railroad crossing, and the old barn. He walked and gazed out over the morning horizon as the sun rose. He saw the glory of both everything and nothing all at once on the golden Texas plains. He walked for a few more miles and hopped a fence to take a shortcut back onto the Reservation. He made it back to his trailer and locked the door behind him and duct-taped bags of ice around his hands and went to bed.

He awoke a couple of hours later to a knock at his door.

Damn, Sunday.

Cady.

He unlocked the door and went to lay back down. She locked the door behind her and greeted him. She saw his hands wrapped up and got his medical supplies out of the cabinet. She said to get up and sit down in a chair so she could see. He mustered up what strength he had and did as she told. She sighed when she saw his face and began to clean his wounds.

"I know it burns," She said.

"You don't have to do this."

"I don't? Holy shit, why didn't you tell me?."

He tried not to laugh so his ribs wouldn't hurt. "Rich bitch."

"Asshole."

They locked eyes for a moment before she refocused, stitching him up. Her eyes were a fierce blue, like a bright Texas sky. "You know you're lucky I'm in nursing now, right?"

"I know."

"You know you could still join me in college, right?"

"No."

"You could. You're smart enough. You got the scholarship. All you have to do is go. Say no to this life. Make something of yourself. You like fighting, so why not be a cop or something?"

"Everyone hates those pigs."

"Dasan," she pleaded. "Listen to me. You don't have to do this. This doesn't have to be your life. There's an entire world out there full of people that need help. And you could help them. You always say fighting is the only thing you're good at, right? Ok, fine. Ain't a damn thing wrong with that, just find something worth fighting for."

"Nothing in this world is worth fighting for."

"Nothing? What about us?" Dasan didn't say anything. "No? Then why do you even fight at all?"

"Because I like it." He said. "I like the challenge."

"Well it may be just a fun challenge for you, but some of us care about things that actually matter."

"So, what I care about doesn't matter?"

She leaned in and kissed his busted lips.

Taste of honey.

"You just care about being challenged? Maybe one day you'll see the biggest challenge in life is giving grace to other people. Especially when they don't deserve it."

She got up and left Dasan sitting alone again.

When he awoke, it was dark outside. He washed and pulled his boots on and started walking back to the bar. When he got there, something was different. Uncle Mato was sitting at a table with some of the other high-ranking Chieftains. Mato's eye was bloody and black. Nobody else was in the bar but them.

The gang had upgraded their traditional peyote for meth-amphetamine in recent years. Some of them were smoking it now. Mato ordered him to sit. Dasan couldn't fathom who would have enough of a death-wish to strike Mato. He sat.

"We have a problem, boy." Mato began. Dasan didn't say anything. "Got some pale-face piece of shit, thinks he can steal from us. Thinks he can beat us, take from us."

"Who?" Dasan asked.

"We don't know yet. But you're gonna find out, and you're gonna peel the top of his head off and bring it to me."

Silence.

"No."

Mato drew a knife and stabbed it into the table.

"I'll fight in this bar all night long, like I always do. But I don't mutilate people."

Mato laughed. "Just what is it gonna take for us to make you a man?" He drew a set of photographs from his jacket and tossed them on the table next to the blade. The photos were of Cady.

"Here's the deal, kid. Every one of us in this room knows all about your sad little crush on that white bitch, Cady Collins. We know she lives at the Green Acres apartments, number 102. We know she goes to church at Grace Fellowship. She drives a blue manual transmission Jeep with a cross hanging on the mirror with Joshua 1:9 engraved on it. She takes nursing classes at the community college four days a week and she waits tables at the Country Café until Sunday, when she comes to waste time with you. Her favorite ice cream is Cherry Amaretto, which you keep in your trailer, just for her."

"She has nothing to do with this."

Mato smirked and continued, "Hell, the only thing we don't know about her is how she looks naked. But I bet we can find out."

Mato's men seized Dasan by the arms before his mangled fists could blacken Mato's other eye. They took him to the ground and beat him unconscious. When he woke up, he had a blade to his forehead. He struck a bargain for Cady's safety. It was the only way.

He said he would find the man who crossed the Chieftains. Who had struck Mato. What he would do once he found him, Dasan didn't know yet. He'd cross that bridge when he came to it.

It took a couple weeks. Dasan was told the man had robbed Mato at gunpoint outside the casino after losing his money in Mato's rigged poker game. Dasan canvassed the local towns and had located a possible match based on Mato's description and the Casino security camera footage he'd been shown, but he wasn't entirely sure. The only name he had learned for the man was "Henry." He appeared to be a manager at a local landscaping company.

Dasan followed him around and learned his schedule, just like Mato had learned Cady's.

A couple days later, Dasan and two senior Chieftains waited for Henry outside his work. One of them went inside and said he needed to make a large order of seed, and that he'd pull his truck behind the building to get it. When Henry came out the back, Dasan and the other gangster beat and restrained him. They took his truck keys and drove him out to the bar and dragged him inside.

Mato tortured him there for hours.

Tied him to a chair. Waterboarded him with whiskey. He

screamed over and over that he had no idea what Mato was talking about. That he had no idea where the money was. Said he had a wife and son. Said he didn't take any money, but he would pay whatever they wanted. Dasan believed him. They had to have the wrong man. No way this guy did it. He was a dorky white dude with glasses and was deaf in one ear. No way he robbed a Chieftain outside a casino at gunpoint and pistol-whipped him upside the head. But Mato said he remembered him from the poker game.

The poker game he was drunk at, no less.

Finally, Mato wiped sweat and alcohol from his face and pulled out a beautiful ceremonial tribal knife. He held it out to Dasan. "It's time," he said. Dasan didn't reply.

Dasan looked at the man.

Henry.

He thought about Cady. His only friend in the world. Her sky-blue eyes. The sweet taste of her honey lips. She was the only good thing to ever happen to him. She wouldn't want him to do this.

But if he didn't, she would find herself in the same chair as Henry. Suffering what would probably be an even worse fate. And Dasan knew he would be made to watch.

Dasan took the knife from Mato.

This was it. Henry or his own uncle.

Dasan could take Mato by surprise.

One way, he could save Cady. The other was a vengeful suicide mission.

He looked Henry in his terrified, desperate eyes, and grabbed him by the hair.

"I'm sorry," he said.

Hunter Fithen is a native Texan writer and avid outdoorsman who has been published in a variety of works, including newspaper articles, small books, and short stories. He currently works full-time as a Texas Peace Officer, where he strives to apply his writing skills to create the world's finest quality police reports.

6 STALL WALK THROUGH

Dean Guell

Sometimes entertainment can come from the strangest of places.

Business equipment wears out over time. An owner must make a decision as to whether the establishment should repair, update, or disband. The choices are not always clear cut. Guesses must be made against upfront costs, operating charges, available labor, interest, and a whole slew of other conditions.

A situation of this sort occurred many years ago to my father. My parents were involved in the dairy farming industry. For a few years, they also grew a few cash crops of peas or sweet corn for a local canning facility.

The farm was located in east-central Wisconsin and in an area known as Kettle Moraine. This location is where the last glacier pushed across the country and melted. The action upon the land and the topography left behind is very mixed. Some hills can be several hundred feet high and flow in contours for several miles. Other hills may be fifteen feet high, three feet wide at the top, and have a base of thirty feet. These hills were created either by the pushing of soil ahead of the approaching glacier or when the glacier stopped moving and the ice melted. The debris within the melting glacier was carried into streams throughout the ice sheet. Eventually the stream and debris would meander to the earth's surface and create the smaller hills. An analogy of what the area appears like from the sky would be if you took a can of worms and poured them out at your feet. The smaller worms would represent the convoluted smaller hills, while the larger piles of worms would represent the massive hills. There are few fields in that area which have two straight edges as outlines. The smaller hills consist of large rocks which have been pushed out of Canada and from the north of the US, and have somewhat of a gravel mix as the major portion of the composition. The shorter and smaller hills have no agricultural value and are ignored when cropping. The area also has numerous small forests or woods with plenty of spring-fed small creeks. The creeks meander around the base of the hills and create additional obstacles for farm machinery.

Dairy barns in that area of Wisconsin were built in respect to the harsh winter climate. Cattle were housed in the lower portion of a structure, while dried feed and bedding were stored overhead. The original barn when my parents milked cows was constructed in the late 1930s. At that time, the structure would have housed about 20 cows plus young stock. Milking was completed by hand in the early years.

In the late 1940s, an addition was added onto the structure. The herd numbers increased to about 45 head, and electricity was used to aid in collecting milk from the cows. The youngstock were moved onto a neighboring farm and housed in a structure constructed with rock and mortar, built before 1930.

Several more additions and changes were added during the 1950s and 1960s. During the late 1970s, the last major changes occurred.

Herd size fluctuated between 60 – 80 cows, depending upon how much labor was available. The later herd size increases, maxed out the physical structure due to the location. The base of a large hill was about ten yards to the east of the barn, and water runoff areas from the hill were located near the south foundation walls. The property line on the north side was about a hundred feet away, and a county road to the west was about a hundred and fifty feet away.

The only possible options for herd increasements were to build something new in another location or to make the existing facility a little bit more efficient. The first option wasn't feasible due to the cost versus return reward.

Another factor under consideration was my father's age, too young to retire, and little desire to carry a huge loan with a 10-13% interest rate.

During the late 1970s, I had the opportunity to work on farms in several foreign countries. These experiences helped to create the next improvement and efficiency on the dairy farm.

During the search to solve the problem of old and deteriorated cow stanchions, inefficient walking paths, and time consumption, we looked at milking parlors to speed the milking process. The introductory costs for the parlor started at $65,000. Removal of old concrete, labor, new concrete, foundations, walls, roofs, electric, and plumbing were all extra. The project wouldn't be feasible after all the expenses were added.

Australia was one of the locations where I was lucky enough to work. One of the farms had a 6-stall walk-through milk parlor. The construction materials between the livestock stalls were of gum lumber, the floor concrete. A simple design with a very low investment cost.

The idea of this style of milking cows was proposed to my father. I had no photos to show, so I had to draw a representation on paper. The idea was a new concept to him, and the proposal needed more study and explanation before any conclusions could be drawn.

The facility in Australia was used for the milking of Jersey cattle; my parents had all Friesian cattle, nearly twice the size of the Jersey breed. Would a walk-through parlor even be feasible with a much larger animal?

The project started by taking physical measures of a small corner in the existing dairy barn. Three six-inch diameter steel posts held up the ceiling and the dry feed storage above the area where this parlor would best fit. These posts could be a major problem.

Having only memory to rely on, from the Australian design, I drew the proposed layout of stall widths, human work areas, livestock flow patterns, milk pipeline patterns, and water lines. The first draft for the project located two of the support posts in undesirable spots.

The project sat for a day or two. I mentioned to my dad that I needed to obtain better numbers for the width and height of a Friesian cow. I needed to measure one of the largest cows in the herd. My dad suggested using an easy to handle cow, an animal which I had taken to the county fair as a calf. The cow was familiar with having a halter on its head, and one could maneuver the creature around a new setting without causing stress to either party. Fortunately, the cow of choice was also one of the largest in the herd.

We corralled the cow after a morning milking period to obtain measurements. The cow was a bit jumpy during the first twenty minutes but soon calmed after her hair was brushed out, and gentle encouragement added.

With accurate data in hand, new drawings were developed. The new drawings became a blessing as the three steel posts were no longer an issue, as they didn't have to be moved from their existing locations. Any necessary water and milk lines were to be placed overhead, so the plumbing of those services would be worked into the picture with ease.

A test stall was needed to make sure the data collected was correct. I sorted through some old lumber which had been saved from an old house tear-down. The full-sized two by fours gathered were to function as the sides of a stall and as a front gate. The friendly cow was coaxed into the strange contraption in exchange for a few tasty protein pellets.

The time came to exhibit the single stall concept to my father. I explained how the other five stalls would fit into the picture and how the cattle would enter and exit the system. Allowances were made for a work area to include a cow trying to bypass the system, or if one needed to be isolated for health reasons. In either case, the function needed to be completed with ease.

The next phase was to determine if any proposed side projects would fit in the chosen area. We had several inches to spare by rearranging two gates on the east side. The extra space was added into the livestock exit walkway.

Old dairy barns in Wisconsin have a gutter which runs behind the cattle to catch waste. The gutter location for the new design would be located in front of the cattle instead of at the rear. The existing location of the gutter became a benefit as we decided to pitch the floor slightly so that any water would run away from the cattle and workers in the milking area. The alignment also eliminated the hassle of young cattle trying to jump over a gutter, causing a splash of waste to everything nearby.

At the time of this project, the milking cattle numbers were around 70. The housing included an enclosed free stall barn. The proposed project needed a system to bring the cattle into the milking area, be milked, then exit with ease. The milked cows had to be separated from the animals yet to be milked.

A feed bunk would segregate the two groups of cattle until the milking process was finished. There was only one narrow livestock entrance door into the structure, so the plan was to create two nine-foot-wide doorways into an existing concrete wall. One doorway would be an entrance for the cattle; the other would become an exit. The same doorways would double as an access point and allow a tractor and loader to push the animal waste from the free stall housing area into the existing gutter after milking hours.

During the entire process, we were frequently visited by supposed experts in the field of milking cows. In reality, they were salespeople, few having ever milked a cow.

My proposed idea was shot down by the professionals for many reasons. The verbiage ran multiple channels and changed with the direction of the wind. A few of the more frequent choices: Jersey cattle don't produce as much milk as Friesian cattle, the climate is different, you won't be able to get the cattle to enter into that design, you're wasting your money, it won't work because no one has ever tried it before, I've never seen or heard of such a thing.

The explanations came swift, were endless, without facts, nor reason.

We smiled and moved ahead with the project.

Upon completion, the first two milking periods required the same amount of time. By the third milking process, the cattle were starting to understand what needed to be done. With each following milking, several minutes were shaved off the clock. By the end of the first week, more than fifteen minutes had been erased from the procedure.

Cleanup time in the free stall barn was also cut by more than twenty minutes for each transaction.

Some of the best savings included the reduction of frustration, exhaustion, and the eliminating of useless tasks.

Six to seven months later, word was out that we had completed the project. One day, we happened to be blessed with a visit from the pundits of gloom. Their wisecracks came fast, but they wished to see the so-called walk through milk parlor.

We were running a normal busy farming operation, but felt no harm in showing the project off. Curiosity overtook the jokes as the scope was viewed.

Milking time was approaching, and one of the parties cautiously asked if they could watch the operation to understand it further.

The milking process had been underway for about three-quarters of an hour when the same bloke inquired about taking pictures.

The walk-through parlor was constructed with new gates and piping, but some items had been secured from salvaged old machinery. A steel L beam had come from the frame of a metal wheeled hay rake, old square-headed bolts were used in place of new stock, small looped chains had been removed from some other equipment, and long orange push bars had come from a corn harvester.

Whispers spread within the group. They departed before the milking was finished for the evening.

We broke out with laughter at the supper table.

About a year and a half later, we attended an Agricultural Field Day. One of the vendors had on display an exaggerated and complicated walk-through parlor. Several visitors were viewing the bells and whistles setup.

We wandered over. A salesperson inquired if we were interested in seeing how the system functioned.

We listened to the sales pitch, nodded, and watched.

The following year, the vendor was out of business.

My father went on to use his walk-through parlor until retirement.

The cost of the homemade parlor, materials, and labor totaled up to less than one-sixteenth of the expert's final quote.

Sometimes previous experiences can lead one through unchartered territory. Great intelligence or funds are not always the best solution when tackling a problem. The issue at hand may consist of a very specific riddle which needs to be solved in an appropriate manner.

Dean writes fiction where real-life situations blend with hopes and dreams. Inspiration, anticipation, and humor may be a part of each journey. Ambiguity allows the reader to decide which part is fact or fiction.

International travel provides scenery settings, while the people of the world provide characters. The merging and mixing of individual parts become the basis of a story.

His early compositions were college material in either creative or technical projects. A continuation of writing skills led to writing instructional information for employees in the food processing fields. Safety documents followed, as did other literary projects.

CHALLENGE

Lynn Harper

He looked at the bright red wrinkled skin. It appeared to glow from within. He carefully cut it in half. He sniffed. Very little smell, interesting. Was that good or bad? Half each, that was the deal. How bad could it be? It didn't matter. He had accepted the challenge and so would win the challenge. He never lost. He put half in his mouth. For one lingering moment, he tasted nothing, then...excruciating pain. The fires of hell reined free in his mouth. He chewed, and each squish between his teeth released more acid onto his tongue. His mind momentarily ejected from his body. He remembered reading about a Roman emperor who had poured molten lead down an enemy's throat. He sympathized with that poor man. He recalled the screaming tortured sinners that burned in hell in renaissance paintings. He knew their pain. He began to repent of the sins he had committed. He asked God to forgive the hubris he had felt just seconds before.

His mind came suddenly back to his mortal body and the white-hot pain in his mouth. He chewed again and more acid burst forth. Out of desperation, he attempted to swallow the half-chewed chunks. He gulped once and forced his Adam's apple to do its job, but his pharynx muscles balked, refusing to complete the task. The burning pieces got caught halfway down his throat. He coughed and gagged, forcing searing juices up into his nasal passages. Tears erupted from his eyes. He hung his head over his plate as snot dripped from his nose. He could feel the acidic fire welling up in his throat, trying to return his mouth. He glanced up and remembered the tall cool glass of milk that he had placed in front of the plate "just in case." His hands shook as he grabbed the glass in both hands and gulped. Sweet relief. The cold milk forced the pieces down. Ah, it was all over. No. A second later the pain roared back unabated. He grabbed some potato chips and crammed them into his mouth, chewing furiously. The salt on the chips just seemed to fuel the flames. He filled his mouth with ice water and lowered the pain momentarily, but he could still feel it smoldering, just waiting for him to swallow. His ears hummed as if he were holding shells up to them and listening to an ocean of pain.

Frantically his mind scrambled for a solution. He remembered as a kid watching his dad use a glass of soda pop to clean battery acid off of the battery terminals on the family sedan. He stumbled to the pantry and grabbed a warm coke. He popped the top and gulped. The coke instantly turned to foam and backed up into his nose. The coke spewed from his nose and mouth as he choked and tried to breathe. He remembered then his childhood amazement at how much the battery terminals had foamed as the soda pop neutralized the acid. Through blurry eyes, he looked across the table at his 10-year-old daughter and saw her grinning face as she laughed and clapped her hands. Her laughter sounded very far away. He resisted the urge to slap her and scrambled for a slice a bread. The bread seemed to tamp down the flames a little. He washed more milk into his mouth and swirled it around, trying to rid every corner of his mouth of the leftover pepper juices that still sizzled. After several minutes of eating bread and drinking milk, the pain finally began to subside. He could still feel an undercurrent of pain that spoke of the dry High Plains summer that had baked the ghost pepper to near-lethal perfection in their small garden. He could still hear a slight buzz in his ears, but he thought he might be able to speak a word or two.

He pushed the remaining half of the ghost pepper toward the young girl and whispered hoarsely, "Your turn."

"Nah, you win again, Dad," she said as she hopped up from the table and skipped off, her ponytail bouncing behind her.

Lynn Harper was raised on the High Plains of Texas before spending seventeen years living in Austin. He moved back to Amarillo with his wife and daughter, where he works as a professional engineer. He earned his engineering degree from Texas Tech University and his MBA from the University of Texas at Austin. Lynn is a beekeeper, a sometimes musician, an avid trail runner and a world traveler.

THE BEAST

Ashley Hendrick

Drool dripped off the fangs of the Beast as it snarled. Rancid breath seeped from its snout like rotten food from a fridge and landed on Amber's nose, but she paid no mind. Her focus was on the Beast's foot. The coarse fur made it hard to wash out the blood, but with a little scrubbing, Amber was able to get most of it off. She dabbed another alcohol swab on the cut, and the Beast snarled again.

"Stop moaning," Amber said. "You're such a baby." She grabbed the Beast's right foot, lifted it, and peered underneath.

"I don't see any more blood," she reassured the Beast. "The skin around your big toe will probably turn black and blue, though."

The Beast glared at Amber and snorted a complaint.

"What did you expect to happen when you kick a door with your bare foot?" She grabbed some gauze and wrapped it around the Beast's big toe. It winced and tried to pull away.

"No, no, no." She pulled it back. "You need to wear this in case it starts bleeding again." Amber carefully and methodically wrapped the Beast's toe tight, making sure no blood could escape.

"Now, let's see how the door is doing?"

The Beast hopped off the bed and meandered with Amber toward her bedroom door. It walked like a gorilla on its fists and stood as tall as one too. Rough, brown fur covered the Beast from head to toe, and it often bumped Amber with its curly ram-like horns. Its snout was as long as a crocodile's mouth with teeth just as sharp. It saw the world through green cat-like eyes that never slept but always searched for trouble. It looked down at the foot of the door.

"Damn." Amber gently rubbed her hand over a small dent at the bottom of the door. "That's kind of impressive, actually." She looked at the muscular creature next to her. If it wanted, it could throw Amber across the room any moment. The Beast had been her constant companion since she was little, and though she could anticipate its tantrums most of the time, it still harbored an unpredictable rage that frightened her. There were moments she couldn't control the Beast. And if she tried, its frenzied outbursts would only worsen. What's more, it never left Amber's side. Even as she slept, she could always feel its presence close by. She would like to say it was watching over her, but as of late, it felt more like it was watching her.

"Let's get ready for tonight."

Amber jumped in the shower, and the Beast followed. Water hit its injured toe, and it yelped. Amber paid no mind. She was too busy thinking about tonight. Who was going to be there? What was she going to say? What was she going to wear? The purple dress. No, too formal. Jeans and a blouse. Shoes? She was planning on wearing her favorite sandals.

As Amber flipped through social scenarios and clothes in her mind, the Beast became agitated. It grunted and slammed its fists against the shower wall.

"Calm down!" Amber said. "It's just a few people Nico knows."

Amber stepped out of the shower and blow-dried her hair. She grabbed a brush and struggled to get her curls out. The Beast did the same with its fur. Amber stopped short and stared at herself in the mirror. This was her first night out in...she couldn't remember how long. This was her chance to change up her look. She could arrive at this party a brand-new person. The Beast looked at her curiously.

Amber reached into a drawer and grabbed the hair iron. The Beast grabbed one too. She let it heat up, grabbed a chunk of curls, and ironed them straight. The Beast did the same. Amber giggled at the Beast's clumsy attempt to straighten its fur, then she looked in the mirror and stopped.

She took a deep breath and closed her eyes.

A loud clapping sound resonated through the bathroom as the Beast threw the iron onto the counter in a sudden fit.

"What the hell?" Amber said. "What's wrong?" The Beast grabbed its own hair and pulled, growling in frustration as it did so. Its fur morphed into sharp, stiff spikes and its eyes turned from meadow green to sheer black. It was losing control.

"You-you don't want to go with straight hair?" It shook its head wildly in an obvious 'No.' "But we could be different for once." She kept her voice calm and quiet. "Don't you want to do something different?"

The Beast reached into a drawer, pulled out a hair tie, and slipped it into Amber's palm. She sighed.

"I don't want to go with a ponytail. I always do that."

The Beast grabbed Amber's brush and smashed it against the counter. The loud cracking noise gave Amber an instant headache, but she refused to back down.

"No," she insisted.

The Beast growled.

"No, no, no."

It roared louder, sending a reverberating rumble through Amber's chest. The brush flew across the bathroom and landed with a plop in the toilet.

Silence fell between them. Amber sighed in defeat.

"Fine. We'll do the ponytail, again." The Beast relaxed and returned to normal. Though Amber was disappointed she wasn't trying something different, she knew the Beast was right. The ponytail was safe and familiar. Not too formal, but not too casual.

"Ber, is everything okay in there?" her brother Nico called from the bottom of the stairs. Amber ran to the door and cracked it open.

"It's fine," she called back. "Just getting ready for tonight."

"Okay." He sounded unconvinced, but Amber ignored it. "Hurry up. We have to stop by the store and grab some beer. Drew and his wife were busy at work all day and forgot to grab some."

"Be down in a minute!"

Amber turned and saw the Beast rummaging through her closet. It pulled out skinny jeans and a blue blouse. Its claws unknowingly threatened to tear the poor shirt. She quickly slipped into the clothes and grabbed her sandals, then thought twice and replaced them with her black flats. She grabbed her phone, stuck it in her back pocket, and ran down the stairs. The Beast followed close behind.

The drive to the party was uneventful, except for the Beast snarling at Nico to slow down on the highway.

"If I want to drive like Granny-Mamma, I'll slow down."

And the Beast relentlessly kicking the back of Ambers seat.

"Ugh, stop! I'll ask him." She turned to her brother. "Nico, did you lock the front door?"

"Yea, I think so."

Another kick.

"Are you sure?"

"No, but it's not a big deal. The thieves will probably only take the TV and the giant vault of millions we have hidden in the basement." He smiled at his sarcasm, and the Beast knocked Nico on the side of the head.

By the time they got to the house, Amber was exhausted from managing the Beast's tantrums.

"You better behave yourself in there," Amber said through gritted teeth as Nico bounded ahead of them to the front door, "or I swear to god, we're never going out again."

Nico didn't bother to knock. He whipped open the door, and a wave of laughter poured out of the house. Amber and the Beast stopped in their tracks. Inside were strangers, people Amber didn't know and who didn't know her, or the Beast.

She took a deep breath and closed her eyes.

The Beast grabbed its horns and shook its head wildly back and forth.

"It's fine. It's fine. It's fine," she reassured it. "They're just people." It grabbed Amber's wrist and squeezed tightly, almost cutting off circulation.

"Ow! Stop! It's only for a few hours." She tried to think of something to say that might calm the Beast. "Maybe somebody brought their own beast with them."

It suddenly stopped shaking and looked at Amber. The thought of someone else having a beast comforted them both. Someone to relate to would be nice.

"C'mon, Ber!" Nico stepped down from the porch and gently grabbed Amber's other wrist. "I'll be with you the whole time."

He ushered them into the house that represented all of Amber's horrors - people. People of every age and size stood in the living room, staring at the newcomers. The Beast turned around and tried to run out the door, but Amber grabbed it by a wad of fur and pulled it back.

"HEY!" Everyone in the room called out in unison. Voices shouted out Nico's name, and people gravitated toward him, slapping him on the back. Amber tried to sink back in the background, but her brother refused to let her.

"This is my little sister, Amber. Amber, this is Drew from Criminology. And this is his wife, Karen. And this is their house."

Drew and Karen introduced themselves to Amber. She refused a beverage and followed Nico further into the hive of gossip and small talk. She shook more people's hands and answered quick, pointless questions.

"How do you like University?"

"What's your major?"

"How have you put up with Nico for so long?"

After 15 minutes of trivial conversation, Amber finally found her way to the couch and sat down, exhausted. She wasn't used to so much socializing. Nor was she used to the eyes of so many strangers looking at her, talking about her, quietly judging her; what she wore, the way she talked, the way she walked, her lack of eye contact. Even as she sat paralyzingly still trying to disappear into the fabric of the couch, she could feel their piercing stares. She could hear them laughing at her awkwardness. The chatter in the room grew louder and louder until Amber could no longer think. She could barely breathe.

Amber took and deep breath and closed her eyes.

Sharp points of needle-like fur poked her arm. She looked next to her at the Beast. Its eyes were black as coal, and it stared, unblinking, straight ahead. A low guttural growl grew from deep in its chest and slowly climbed up its throat. Its lips curled up to bare its fangs, and the growl escaped, inviting more stares and whispers from the strangers.

Amber froze.

What was the Beast about to do? What chaos was it planning to release on these people? She had to keep the Beast from ruining the party and her night. She gently grabbed the Beast's hand to distract it. It paid no mind. It continued to growl and stare.

Karen walked past, and Amber quickly asked where the bathroom was. Before she could finish giving directions, the Beast bounded up the stairs toward the bathroom. Amber followed close behind.

"What are you doing?" Amber asked as she locked the door behind them. "What's going on?"

The Beast seemed to have grown twice its size in the time it took to run up the stairs. It towered over the sink and stared into the mirror, panting against its reflection with its sour breath. It gripped the sides of the sink so tight, Amber thought it might crack.

"They're just people," Amber said. "What are you so afraid of?"

It snarled and yanked the handles of the faucet back and forth, turning the water on and off, on and off and on. The water ran down the Beasts arm like a stream careening through a forest. Amber gasped in shock as a splash of cold water hit her face.

"What the hell?" she said.

Jewelry and medicine bottles fell to the floor as the Beast bolted from the sink to the toilet. It whipped the seat up and threw it back down with a loud thwack, over and over again.

Thwack, thwack, thwack.

"STOP IT!" Amber pleaded.

The Beast reached for a roll of toilet paper and squeezed so hard Amber was sure it was going to rip in half. A roll flew across the bathroom toward her head. Then another, and another. She tried to dodge them all as she leaped toward the Beast. She wrapped her arms around its giant torso like a human straight jacket, but to no avail. It vaulted off the toilet, kicked the bottom of the bathroom door, and howled in pain.

"Stop kicking doors! Somebody's going to come up here!"

It roared in response and slapped its hands against the wall. The Beast stomped furiously across the room toward Amber, terror and frustration in its wake. She stumbled backward against the wall. This was it. It was over. She had lost all control over the creature and it knew it. She turned away as the Beast let out a deafening roar in her face, animosity dripping from its fangs.

"Please," Amber quietly begged. "Stop."

It looked down at Amber and breathed heavily. It wasn't ready to stop.

Voices on the other side of the door. The Beast suddenly covered its ears and threw itself down on the floor, wailing in distress. It didn't want any more people, or judging, or gawking. It banged its fists against the tiled floor as hard as it could.

Amber fell on top of the Beast and held it. Its fur relaxed to its normal texture, but she could still feel the Beast shaking.

Its breathing was short and labored as if it struggled to breathe at all. It was scared. Low sobs came from somewhere deep inside the Beast, and it began to cry.

"Ber? Are you okay?" Nico's voice sounded through the door, and he tried to open it. "Amber, let me in."

There were scuffling and whispers on the other side. Metal slid into metal and the door opened. Nico walked in slowly, tiptoeing over the toilet paper and jewelry. He turned the running water off and knelt next to his crying sister. He placed a gentle hand on her back. Through her sobs, she heard him whisper what she wanted to hear for the past half hour.

"Let's go home."

The car was silent on the way home. Nico didn't ask about what happened in the bathroom, and Amber didn't tell him. Her eyes were still raw from crying and most of her energy on the way home was spent trying to block out the memory of the night.

When they got home, Amber went upstairs and into her room. She closed the door, turned on the light, and looked around for a moment. It was quiet, almost serene. Amber slipped into her pajamas and sat on her bed. She looked down at her feet.

Amber put her right foot on the bed and unwrapped the bloody bandages on her big toe. She was right. It was already starting to turn black and blue.

Ashley Hendrick is a teacher, journalist, and juggler. She loves to travel to far off lands and learn anything and everything she can. Her hobbies include reading, writing, watching every movie ever made, and playing the occasional song on her ukulele. She is also a freelance photographer and videographer and has been both a reporter and editor for The Prairie Newspaper. Ashley currently resides in Amarillo, Texas, where she dreams of reaching grown-up goals but secretly wants to join the circus.

THE HOODED WAY

Lynnette Jalufka

J oyful music filled the hall of Mardon Castle. Guests conversed with each other as they ate wild boar and drank wine. A horn called the revelers to attention as Lord Gavin stood at the table on the dais. "My lords and ladies, 'tis good for you to join me on this Adam the Small Day, the most important day of the year for Mardon Castle. Without Adam's courage, I wouldn't be standing before you now. I give you Will the Minstrel to remind us why we celebrate this day every summer."

He gestured to a middle-aged man with balding hair as he sat down. Will ambled into the center of the hall, a lute strapped around his back. "Thank ye, milord," he said as he bowed with a dramatic wave of his hand. He took off the lute and strummed his fingers along the strings of the instrument. "Now lend an ear, ye good gentles. 'Tis time for the story of Adam the Small."

Twilight cast a purple hue over Mardon Castle, but the warm hall was drenched with despair. Squire Adam stood by Sir Robert, watching the other occupants in the torchlight. Lord Faukes paced upon the rushes on the floor. Against the wall sat his daughter, Brianna, head buried in her hands, with her mother's arm around her shoulders.

The sound of her sobbing wrenched Adam's heart. Had Lord Faukes' knights been able to best Lord Umbray's in the tournament melee the day before, this would not have happened. If Faukes didn't get drunk and wager his daughter to Umbray, Brianna would be her usual jubilant self. If Adam had been allowed to fight...

But, no. That could not be. He would never be knighted. Lord Faukes had said he had no use for a knight of such short stature. He even laughed at Sir Robert's recommendation. Never mind that Adam could best his fellow squires that towered over him. So, at five and twenty years, he was doomed to be a squire forever.

Brianna was different, being the only one in the castle who encouraged him, besides Sir Robert. "Don't listen to them," she had said when others pierced him with their jests. "You're just as good." Her words were like a honey balm that soothed his misery, and her smile illuminated his darkest hours.

How he wished he could marry her! But such a lady would not consent to a lowly squire, especially one so small. Nor would her father agree to such a match.

A servant ran into the hall and bowed before Faukes. "Lord Umbray is here, my lord. He wants to collect his prize."

Faukes slowly nodded. "Let him in."

Brianna's head sprang up, her beautiful face marred by streams of tears.

Lord Umbray marched into the hall, followed by his retinue. He was a massive pig of a man; Adam felt sorry for his horse. If Umbray would have fought in the melee, his men would have lost. Bits of food and grease littered his black beard. But he carried himself like a king, with jewels adorning his fingers, belt, and scabbard.

Faukes smiled at his guest. "Lord Umbray, this is an unexpected—"

"Surely, you haven't forgotten our bargain, Faukes," Umbray said, his tiny black eyes on Brianna. "I'll take her now."

"At this hour? It is late. Come, stay the night. Enjoy my hospitality. Then you will be refreshed for your ride back on the morrow."

Umbray raised an eyebrow. "How do I know you won't hide her away somewhere?"

"I keep my word, Umbray. She will be ready on the morrow."

"She'd better be." He snapped his fingers at Brianna. "Come here, wench."

Brianna gave her father a questioning look. Faukes lowered his head and turned away. She glared at him, lips in a thin line, as she slowly rose from her chair and walked to the bulging lord, her head high.

When she came near, Umbray grabbed her arm and dragged her to his barrel chest. The monster was easily four times her size. "She'll do," he said, stroking her golden hair with his other hand.

"Please let go, my lord," Brianna pleaded. "Your grip is too tight."

"Oh, is it?" Umbray said maliciously. "Get a priest. I'll wed her now."

Hot blood pounded through Adam's veins. "Let her go!" he shouted before he realized what he was saying.

"Who said that?" Umbray bellowed.

Heads turned toward Adam. He swallowed as he stepped forward. "I did, milord."

"And you are?"

"Just Sir Robert's squire, who doesn't know his place," Faukes answered. "Pay him no heed."

Umbray gave a hearty laugh. "A mere boy thinks to give me orders?"

Adam's chest burned as if it contained a bonfire. "I'm no boy. I'm five and twenty. And since you like wagers, milord, I propose a challenge. If I win, Lady Brianna is free from your deal with Lord Faukes and can marry anyone she chooses."

"I love a wager, especially when I can't lose," Umbray

beamed. "I accept. You will face Sir Langley."

Adam gazed at the tall, scar-faced knight standing by Umbray. His throat went dry. He had hoped to fight the fat pig. Sir Langley was undefeated in tournaments. To fight him would mean certain death.

The knight growled, "I'll gladly show this insolent pup his place, my lord. What's your challenge, squire?"

Adam took a deep breath. He couldn't stop now, not with Brianna's future at stake. He looked up into the steel eyes of the champion and said, "A race, a horse race through the Hooded Way."

"A horse race?" Sir Langley laughed. "And what's this Hooded Way?"

"'Tis a hunting path through the wood around the castle."

"It's foolishness!" cried Langley. "Bah! We should settle this with arms."

Adam half-smiled. "Sir, if you think the challenge too difficult—"

"Too difficult? I'll win, you brazen cur. My best courser is with me. Batolf is the fastest horse in the land."

Umbray slapped Faukes' back. "What say you, Faukes?"

Faukes nodded slowly.

"Then it's done," Umbray said. "The race will be set at sunrise. Then we can be on our way with the maid." He released Brianna so quickly that she spun in a circle. Adam ran to her aid, steadying her before she fell.

"Thank you," she said, rubbing her arm. "That was very brave. I know you can win."

His voice deserted him as he looked at her face, still red, but bright with hope. He only nodded as her mother led her away. Forget the race; Adam could soar to the moon and back with that one glance.

Sir Robert pulled him aside. "You can't gallop through the Hooded Way, Adam. You know that."

Adam grinned. "But Sir Langley doesn't. I've ridden there many times. I know the way."

Then God be with you."

The sun barely peeked over the horizon as the guests and inhabitants of the castle gathered in the courtyard. Adam rode his bay horse, Crispin. Langley pranced beside him on the black Batolf. Mounted, the knight still towered over Adam. If Crispin ran as fast as Adam's beating heart, they would win for sure.

Brianna came toward him, carrying a long blue ribbon. A rock lodged in his throat, preventing him from greeting her. She was as radiant as the rising sun, much improved from the previous evening. "Adam, will you wear my favor?"

He cleared his throat. "'Tw-'twill be my pleasure, milady," he squeaked as he leaned down.

"Thank you for doing this," she said as she tied the ribbon around his upper arm. "Godspeed, Adam."

A smile covered his face. He could fly through the Hooded Way by himself.

"We're wasting time!" Umbray's voice boomed. "I want to be on my way."

Brianna jumped, then hurried to her parents.

"The first one through the castle gates wins," Faukes said weakly. He nodded to his daughter. Brianna took out another ribbon and raised her arm.

"Get on with it!" Umbray shouted. He grabbed her arm, forcing it down.

Adam glared at the fat pig. But hoofbeats echoed off the wooden drawbridge. Langley had already started! Adam was behind. He spurred Crispin out of the castle and onto the road. He had to catch up; Brianna's life depended on it.

Langley had a ten-length lead when Adam watched him disappear into a hole that opened in the wood. Adam followed him into the darkness of the Hooded Way. The path was so named for the branches that intertwined with each other, forming a tightly knit canopy over the trail. Many hung low; some had fallen and laid across the path. Everything was shaded except where sunlight lanced through the full leaves of summer.

Adam slowed Crispin as much as he dared. Though he was

small enough to fit underneath the branches, he still had to be alert.

Crack! Whoosh! Thud!

Adam followed the path in the direction of the sounds. He found Langley sitting on the ground beneath a low branch, moaning. Adam suppressed a grin; his plan had worked. But he couldn't leave an injured knight alone in the Hooded Way. "Sir, are you hurt?"

Langley struggled to his feet. His eyes shot arrows at Adam. "You conniving knave! You knew that branch was there. And you could fit under it!"

"You agreed to the challenge, Sir Langley."

"Face me like a man, you coward! I'll slit you like the rabbit you are."

Obviously, the knight needed no help. Adam kicked Crispin, and they continued along the path. They found Batolf, nibbling at the undergrowth by a tree. The horse was unfortunately too close to where Langley fell. Rustling leaves and snapping twigs indicated the knight was stomping through the wood. Adam had to hurry.

The Hooded Way seemed more treacherous this time. The branches hung lower than he remembered, causing him to bend over Crispin's neck. Limbs littered the path, which made Crispin trot more than canter, with the occasional jump over a fallen branch. Even pierced with sunlight, the shaded darkness pressed upon them. The Way seemed to last an eternity.

Crashing and cursing came from behind. Adam glanced back to see Langley gaining on him. Just then, Crispin jumped over a log, and a branch hit Adam's head. He fought to stay in the saddle. Once he settled Crispin, something wet slid down his cheek. He touched it with his fingers. Blood.

"I'll break your neck, you hapless worm!" Langley bellowed with the hiss and clunk of a sword upon wood. The knight was using his weapon to chop through the branches.

Adam drove his heels into Crispin, and on through the gloom they went. Finally, a round opening of light emerged ahead. The end of the Way! With one last jump, they entered blinding sunlight. Now Crispin could gallop! With all the strength he had in his legs, arms, and body, he urged the horse faster.

Langley thundered after them like an approaching storm. "You'll wish your mother never gave you birth!"

Adam dared not look back. "Haste, Crispin, haste!" They reached the drawbridge; Crispin's hooves hammered the planks only a moment before Batolf's.

Crispin led by a neck when they passed through the gates to the cheers of the crowd. The next thing Adam knew, he was on the ground, with a great weight on top of him, forcing the air from his lungs. He could see nothing but white stars. Pain ran through his shoulder.

The weight came off. "Get up!" Langley jerked Adam to his feet by his hair. Blood ran down his lip; his nose was bleeding. His feet danced beneath him for balance. He stared up into the knight's face, cold as steel.

Langley's eyes bore into Adam's. "Now, we'll see what you're really made of."

"Peace, Langley," Sir Richard intervened. "Let him go. The race is over, and you lost."

"But the little rat tricked me into going through a path only he could fit." He shook the squire as he spoke. Adam gritted his teeth.

"He won, and we are all witnesses," Sir Richard said. "That's what you agreed to. Let him go."

Langley scowled before tossing Adam back on the dirt as if he was a scrap of meat thrown to a hound. The squire laid there, catching his breath.

"Adam won, Lord Umbray," Faukes said, the corners of his mouth curled upward. "You and your men can now be on your journey."

Umbray rounded on him. "Did you think I would leave without my bride?"

Faukes stood straight. "You won her in a wager, and you

lost her in a wager. You have nothing to complain about."

"We'll see about that." He stepped toward Brianna.

Ignoring his aching body and dripping nose, Adam scrambled to his feet and placed himself in front of the oversized pig. His sword hissed as he drew it. "You'll never get Lady Brianna!"

"Your wit won't deny me my prize, stupid pup," Umbray smirked. His hand went to his sword, but as he yanked it out, he stumbled to his right.

Adam pushed the lord's left side with all his might. Umbray landed on his back, shaking the earth. Adam placed a foot on the lord's sword hand and aimed his blade at Umbray's throat.

Pointed steel surrounded the squire, from both Faukes' and Umbray's men. Adam paid no heed. "Call off your men, milord, and be gone. Your business here is concluded."

"Do as he says, you idiots!" Umbray shouted. "Stand down!" His men obeyed; their blades were sheathed. But Faukes' men kept theirs out.

"Now go and gamble on another lady," Adam said as he released Umbray.

Umbray glared at him as his men helped him up. "Very well, I'll go. A wager is a wager." He stomped toward his waiting horse and rode out of the castle without another word, taking his retinue with him.

The castle inhabitants erupted into praise. "Huzzah for Adam the Small! Huzzah, Adam, huzzah!"

"Well done, Adam." Sir Richard patted him on the back.

Adam wiped the blood from his face. "Thank you, Sir."

"Well done, indeed," Faukes said. He rubbed his chin. "Is it not time you were knighted?"

Adam beamed. "Knighted?" But he had no time to say anything else as Brianna filled his vision. She threw her arms around his neck and surrounded his mouth with her soft lips.

That was all the reward he needed.

Clapping echoed off the walls as Will the Minstrel finished

his tale. Lord Gavin rose from his chair. "Thank you, Will. Now everyone raise your goblet in honor of my great-grandfather, Adam the Small, who proved wit and courage matter more than a man's stature."

Lynnette Jalufka has written stories since she was a little girl growing up in Texas. Her short story, "Reining in a Dream," was published in With Words We Weave: Texas High Plains Writers 2019 Anthology. She is an experienced horsewoman who has shown horses for many years. She also enjoys reading historical and adventure books as well as singing in her church choir. A fan of the Middle Ages with its armored knights and their magnificent mounts, she is currently working on a medieval fantasy series. You can read her weekly blog about writing every Saturday at wordsmithsix.com.

THE CHOICE

Audrey Cannady Massingill

As the first Christmas after my father's death approached, Mother and I were still living with the grief and fear which had been with us since our loss six months before.

We both knew Christmas would never be the same. Daddy would not come home early in the morning from his job at the tavern with presents hidden under his coat. There would be no tall tree in the corner with the familiar ornaments clustered on the branches. Mother couldn't afford the ingredients to bake a dozen kinds of cookies.

The previous Christmas, the three of us, Daddy, Mother, and I had been together in our house on Douglas Avenue. Early in January 1951, my father had gone to Barnes Hospital in St. Louis, and Mother and I had moved into Aunt Annie Boad's house on Grand Avenue. My grandfather Muskopf and Mother's youngest sister, Aunt Julia, and her five (soon to be six) children were already living in the small four-room house. After my father died in May, the ten of us moved into Grandpa Muskopf's home on Union Avenue, where all three of my mother's brothers were already entrenched.

Even though four adults and seven children were crowded into Grandpa's four-room house, Mother and I felt alone. Her pride would not allow her to ask for help from anyone who would have been able to assist us in making the transition from our previous cherished state to our now bleak existence.

Mother was only forty years old, and I was ten, but the loss of my father had aged us beyond our years. We felt old and tired. And scared.

Mother had gone from her father's home to her husband's house and had no experience making decisions beyond what to cook for supper that evening. She had never handled money. Daddy had always taken care of us. Daddy had had a life insurance policy, but after paying for his medical bills and the funeral, there was nothing left. Even receiving our whole income on a monthly basis from Social Security rather than a weekly allowance from Daddy was an almost insurmountable obstacle for my mother. If we received all of our income only once a month, how were the weekly expenses for groceries to be paid beyond the first week?

Mother was overwhelmed with fears and worries, and I took my attitude from her.

Two weeks before Christmas, Mother decided she had to do something to lift our spirits. She asked Uncle Theron, her youngest brother, to take us to St. Louis for a day of Christmas shopping.

"I'll be glad to go with you, Minnie," Uncle Theron said, "but I won't drive over there." Although it is not that far, going to St. Louis was always a big event, and many Bellevilleans, even now, are apprehensive about driving in the Big City.

"That's okay," Mother told him. "I'm just worried about Audrey and me going over there by ourselves. What if we got lost or I got my purse stolen?"

"We'll go Saturday and make a day of it," my uncle promised.

On Saturday morning, we were up early, and by eight a.m.,

the three of us were standing across the street waiting for the Raab Avenue bus, which would take us to The Square at downtown Belleville where we would catch the bus to St. Louis.

The day was crisp and cold, the wind was soft, and there was a hint of moisture in the air. A perfect winter day.

Downtown St. Louis was magical for Christmas. Stix, Baer & Fuller and Famous & Barr were the biggest stories, each taking up a whole square city block. The store windows were decorated with animated Christmas scenes. Santas turned and waved at us. Little elves tapped their hammers on the toys they were making. Ballerinas twirled. Electric trains ran round and round on elaborate sets of tracks. Christmas carols were piped into the air.

We spent the morning look at all the lovely gifts in the stories and then headed for the bargain basement at Famous & Barr. The bottom floor of the store was filled with inexpensive things that we could afford, and we managed to get a gift for everyone. I had Uncle Theron distract Mother while I bought a box of lacy handkerchiefs for her.

At noon my uncle led us through a maze of side streets to a cafeteria for lunch. I had never been to a smorgasbord, as we called a buffet, and couldn't choose what to eat from all of the dishes set out.

"Get a little of everything," Uncle Theron advised. "This is my treat."

After stuffing ourselves with turkey and all the things that go with it, we ended our meal with big slabs of chocolate pie.

Leaving the cafeteria, we ambled down the street. It was still early, and although we had finished our shopping, we didn't want to go home just yet.

"Let's go to the show," Uncle Theron said. So we walked over to the Fox Theater, where they were playing *King Solomon's Mines*.

The Fox had just installed a wide screen so they could show the new Cinemascope movies. The film started, and soon we were deep in the African jungle with Stewart Granger and Deborah Kerr. The huge screen made us feel as if we were right there with them.

When we came out of the theater, three hours later, the light was fading, and it was colder. It was time to go home. We were tired and didn't talk much on the long bus ride to Belleville.

After that day in St. Louis, Mother and I felt better than we had all year. It seemed to me that the dazed, lost look in her eyes had lightened.

The following week, we bought a small tree from the Boy Scout's lot on Freeburg Avenue and decorated it with some of our favorite ornaments. I remember how brightly that Christmas tree shone on the table in our room. We wrapped our gifts in colorful paper that Mother had saved from the year before. After they were arranged under the tree, I had a good time dropping hints to my cousins about their presents while they tried to guess what could be in the packages.

Mother baked a batch of our traditional Christmas sugar cookies in the shapes of Santa, stars, and Christmas trees. She decorated them with colored icing and red hots. On Christmas Eve, my cousins and I had big, juicy tangerines after supper. A rare treat.

Before we went to bed, I stood in front of the tree and laid my chin on the table. With my eyes half-shut, I peeked inside the stable at the tiny baby Jesus and his family. The nativity scene was the same as it had always been. It had not changed.

I thought about the past year and realized that even though everything was different now, it was up to me to shape this new life. Although I could not put it into words, I knew that no matter what the future held for me, I had the power within myself to make my life happy or sad. The choice was mine.

The choice will always be mine.

Audrey Cannady Massingill was born in Belleville, Illinois. She moved to Texas in 1960 and came to Amarillo in 1982. Audrey enjoys genealogy research and writing. She writes about her family and growing up among a large cast of aunts, uncles, and cousins. She has self-published several genealogy books, family story books, and memoir. During this time of shelter-in-place, she has finished her final book of stories about growing up in Belleville and a sort-of comic book inspired by a trip to Cape Cod last year featuring the adventures of The Caped Cod and his trusty sidekick, Underdog. This story, The Choice, won second prize at the Abilene (Texas) Writers Guild contest, Inspiration Category, 2006.

FOOTPRINTS ON
THE HEART

Phyliss Miranda

One Spring Night
Small Town, Texas

T he night was enchanting...the most wonderful evening Felicia and Robby had ever experienced. The stars in the heavens looked as if they had been sprinkled throughout the skies just for them, announcing to the world tomorrow would be their wedding day.

Felicia and Robby embraced, entranced in one another's arms, letting their feet glide them gracefully across the floor. Their bodies moved to the music as if they were one.

Robby looked incredibly handsome in his uniform, so tall and authoritative.

Felicia's evening gown hugged her summer tan, making it appear as if snow showers had fallen on her shoulders and sent an avalanche of white flakes down the back of her voluptuous body.

"Felicia, thank you for the most incredible evening of my

life," Bobby whispered in her ear. "I don't want this evening to ever end, but we have to leave for work soon." He pulled her closer into his arms. "Tonight is going to be difficult, just thinking about you and how beautiful you are," he finished as he whirled her off the dance floor.

Wishing everyone a good night, Felicia hurriedly took Robby by the hand and lead him toward her car. She gave him a kiss and started the car engine. She quickly said, "Robby, please be careful. There are a lot of crazies out there."

Suddenly she stopped and added, "Hey, guy, I love you to the moon and back."

Driving home, Felicia couldn't help but think how unusually heavy the traffic seemed. When she arrived at her small apartment, she quickly changed into the new white scrubs she had purchased just for the night before her wedding. She thought it fitting that the bride should wear white. She pulled on her jacket and adjusted the ties on the waist of her pants, then headed out the door so she wouldn't be late for her shift at the local hospital.

"Tonight is my lucky night," she whispered out loud as she pulled into a premium parking space and headed to the emergency room entrance.

Her thoughts were abruptly interrupted by the only too familiar sound of the dispatcher calling a Code 4 incoming ambulance with an ETA of four minutes. As the Unit Clerk wrote Trauma Room #3 on the whiteboard, Felicia's hopes that this would be a slow night in the ER were brushed aside. She prepared to begin work on the incoming patient. Closing her locker, she rushed down the hall to the trauma rooms.

In the still of the night, she heard the sirens of the approaching ambulance. They came to a standstill. Shortly the automatic doors burst open and the paramedics rushed in with the patient, followed closely by two ashen-faced police officers. Both she knew, but had a job to do and swiftly brushed past the officers in the direction of Trauma Room #3, not particularly noticing the shocked look on the men's faces.

Felicia reached the room only to be promptly held back by her friend, Carolyn, who told her she couldn't come in. Confused, Felicia pulled away from her fellow nurse in order to get a good look at the patient.

Nausea soured her stomach, making her lose focus on the patient being transferred from the gurney to the examining table. Her limbs became increasingly weak, making her unsteady on her feet. Her heart pounded profusely. All of her years as a nurse had not prepared her for the bitterness of tragedy. She realized right away this was no exception. One could never get used to the sadness of what she witnessed day in and day out.

Felicia couldn't hear the scream coming out of her own mouth. "Oh God, it's Robby. It's Robby," she sobbed…something any nurse would never allow herself to do.

Time suspended around her as she watched the trauma team work on her beloved Robby, knowing she shouldn't be even near the room, much less right inside. She had to be there.

To her ears the words, "Felicia, honey, it isn't good for you to be here…. You know the rules, you can't work on a loved one".

"Please, please, Felicia, we'll let you know something as soon as possible." She was swiftly ushered out the door by a faceless person and handed off to one of the police officers. She crumbled into his arms, the coolness of his badge embedded in her tear-stained cheek.

Softly, she inquired, "What happened, Hank?"

Hank explained that when Robby exited the gate of the Country Club on a routine call, a drunk driver came over the hill at a high rate of speed and rammed Robby's unit, trapping him inside. The jaws of life were used to extrapolate him.

Traumatized beyond belief, Felicia leaned against the transport gurney outside Trauma Room #3, watching as her friends continued to work on Robby.

Minutes turned into hours.

She stared at her hands…the hands that had helped save so many lives, unable to help the one person she loved more than life. Felicia continued to watch as routine procedures were followed, knowing he was in capable hands, but also knowing the magnitude of his injuries.

Felicia kept her eyes glued in the direction of Trauma Room #3, only being able to see Robby's feet as he was encircled with medical personnel, the people she would be working with if it were any other patient. She continued looking at Robby's feet; they were so swollen, so ashen, so lifeless. She knew what the signs meant.

Her silence was startled back to the moment as she heard the attending physician say, "Time?" She knew only too well the meaning of the request. She jerked her head toward the clock she'd watched for so many hours. From inside, she heard, "3:06". It was over, they would begin removing their gloves, gowns, masks, and caps, pausing for silent prayers, shaking their heads, while exhaustion and the cloak of disappointment engulfed them...knowing they had done everything possible and wishing they could have done more. Feelings she had shared more times than she wished to remember.

In the back of her mind, she heard the sirens of the next emergency arriving at their doorsteps.

The attending physician, Dr. Jeffers, emerged from the room, on his way to the incoming patient, and briefly stopped to offer his condolences.

"I'm so sorry, Felicia, they'll have the room ready in short order, so you can go back in," his face said it all.

"No, I want to go in now," she whispered as she walked aimlessly toward the door.

Robby's torn uniform lay on the floor in the corner, his pants and shirt having been cut off. A procedure way too familiar to her. One shoe conspicuously lay next to the shirt, disjointed, as if it didn't belong with the uniform.

Felicia entered the room as if she were a first time visitor, observing things as though she had never seen them before... particularly the cold, stark examination table where the lifeless body of her beloved laid.

As calm as she could muster up, she took his hand in hers,

tenderly kissed it, not caring that her new uniform was being smeared with his blood. She softly laid her head on his chest and allowed all of her bottled-up emotions to explode, ending with a prayer for her beloved Robby.

Knowing Trauma Room #3 would need to be used soon, she composed herself and began to straighten the blanket covering his body. On top of the neatly folded blanket, she placed his arms...the arms that only hours before held her so tightly. She kissed his unresponsive lips.

"I love you so much and always will," she said as if he was sleeping and he would awaken, look into her eyes, and hold her tight after his nap.

Finally leaving her beloved fiancé, she heard people talking but had no idea what they said. She responded, not knowing what she even said. Everyone was talking in slow speed, reminding her of the times when she was young and played a 45 RPM record at 33 1/3 RPM.

Everything was in slow motion. She heard another siren from far away. The dispatcher writing GSW coming with ETA 2 minutes, Trauma Room 6. The squeak of the marker on the whiteboard sounded like fingernails scratching a chalkboard.

Not bothering to clock out, she left the hospital, not knowing where she was going, but knowing she had to get away from all of the madness, the nonsense.

Felicia didn't remember getting into her car nor arriving at the sight of Robby's accident. Her heart was too heavy to even care where she was or where she was going. Light showers began to fall as she pulled her car to the side of the road. She sat there for a long time, just looking out of the windshield, watching the wipers swishing back and forth, in cadence, as if they were soldiers marching off to war.

The wreckage had been carefully cleaned up with little reminder that such a tragedy had just taken place. The only evidence of the accident were tiny shattered glass fragments and small crushed red taillight pieces that had been swept toward the side of the road. The full moon illuminated them as if they were diamonds and rubies resting on a bed of asphalt.

Felicia walked around along the side of the road. It was so quiet, so serene. The wildflowers looked as if they were drooping their faces in shame, closing their petals for the night, covering their faces to shield themselves from the tragedy of the evening. She noticed something shiny and black amongst the wildflowers. She reached for it and realized it was Robby's missing shoe. She crushed it in her chest, feeling his warmth, as she continued to sit on the side of the road, feeling close to Robby.

A car door opened in the distance. She barely heard it softly close, and the slow shuffling of footsteps approaching her until she felt the warmth of a friendly hand was on her shoulder. She looked up into the eyes of Sgt. Hank Hudson, Robby's partner...his mentor...his friend.

"Hi, Kid, I figured you'd be here. Thought you could use a little of this." He removed the pull tab from a cup of steaming coffee.

Felicia felt so thankful for his show of kindness and accepted the cup without releasing her hold on Robby's shoe.

Words were unspoken as moments passed in silence. She simply thanked him for the coffee. The friends sat on the curb, each absorbed in their own thoughts.

"Hank," she finally began, "I loved him so much."

"I know, Kid, we all did," the surly old lawman said, obviously holding back his anguish, trying to conceal his vulnerable side, trying to shield himself from the hurt he felt so deeply. The side of him she knew he could only share with her.

They continued to sit on the roadside, their thoughts only occasionally interrupted by the lights of an oncoming car over the hill. Felicia finished the coffee, placed the paper cup on the ground between them as if it were a fine china cup.

The sun peeked its sleepy face over the hills as Robby's long-time partner and superior officer took Felicia gently by the hand and escorted her to her car.

Without words, they each knew they had lost a part of the lives.

Something that could never be replaced, realizing that Robby would never be forgotten, as he had left footprints on their hearts.

A native Texan, *New York Times* and *USA Today* award-winning author Phyliss Miranda has been an active member of Panhandle Professional Writers d/b/a Texas High Plains Writers for two decades. She enjoys sharing her love of the new frontier, particularly the Texas Panhandle, and still believes in the Code of the West. Visit her at phylissmiranda.com.

Note from the author. This was the first story I wrote over two decades ago as an assignment when I took my first writing class from Jodi Thomas. Our project was to write a short story about "a shoe on the side of the road." It's rough and tough, but hopefully shows the reader how I changed as a writer with the help of my friends and colleagues in PPW.

THE SECOND PROPOSAL

Ashlyn Parker

He reaches over and grabs her hand.

He has wrinkled, rough fingers and even some missing tips from a woodshop accident back in high school. These fingers join with her wrinkled but soft hands from years of routinely washing dishes followed by Aloe Vera lotion.

For nearly 60 years, these hands have held together - from the time he serenaded her with Johnny Cash songs played on his guitar, through dozens of handwritten love letters. These hands joined for good the day they eloped in Mexico. They held tight during the period he used a welding rod, to when she held their two children. Then their grandchildren. Then their great-grand-child.

He leads her down the hallway of their home, lined with framed pictures of far-away family members. He wants no one to hear what he has to say next.

He closes the door behind him but never lets go of her hand.

He turns to face her. His brown eyes are framed with fine smile lines from years of cracking jokes. Hers are light blue and lined with white eyelashes behind delicate glasses.

He drops her hand and cups her face.

His expression softens in a way she rarely saw in the leader of her family.

After a moment of confused, intimate silence, he whispers...

"Will you marry me?"

Her eyes well. This feels more romantic than the first time he proposed. But overall bittersweet, because it's another memory robbed by disease.

Her husband doesn't look much different. He is the same man weathered by age and years of hard, hard labor. His smile is the same one that has graced her across the breakfast table over bowls of Cheerios.

What's changed the most is his mind.

Some days he wants to leave. Their home is no longer his. He longs for his childhood home in New Mexico, back with his mother and brother, who have both been gone for decades.

Other days, he wonders who the bossy red-headed woman is in their house, and "just who does she think she is?"

On good days, he returns to his artistic abilities and uses colored pencils to bring life to coloring books.

On bad days, he hunts for the things people have "taken" from him in the night. He sees them rummaging through his things, so he hides his treasured coin collection. Buffalo nickels and wheat head pennies can be found throughout the house... which sadly turns into a daily valuable Easter egg hunt.

In some ways, many things HAVE been taken from him over the years. Things that were once so important to him, like his truck keys. He longs to carry on his usual errands of gathering the mail or crossing off his wife's grocery list. Those joys were taken from him after an awkward family intervention.

He feels as though the doctor diagnosed him as crazy. He will never forgive his wife for scheduling that appointment. He thinks, at least.

He struggles to let his son take over tasks he once did

without a problem. He was a man whose pastimes required power tools to build houses and really anything he imagined. He could take a block of wood and whittle a toy gun for his grandson or a cat figurine for his granddaughter with a simple pocket knife. He still feels like he can refinish antique furniture and mow the lawn, even though his wife has to help him dress every day.

But as the tears roll down her cheeks, she whispers a "yes" to his proposal. Even though she didn't understand the words "for better or worse" uttered in Spanish during their elopement, she meant it.

She still loves the man in front of her, even though he is much different than the man to whom she vowed.

He still makes her laugh every day with his witty comments. He still brushes her hair back with his hands and tells her frequently how much he loves her. He brags to visitors that "she's the one." There's no place he would rather be than in the same room as her, and even though she is not used to him as her shadow, she has learned to cope with no alone time.

She has learned to cope with each key ability that slips away without notice. She tells her family she will cope for as long as she physically and mentally can, and fight the temptation to surrender him to caretakers.

She can't imagine sending away the man who dedicated his life to her: from the time they lived in an empty rental house playing checkers, to their three-story home filled with lavish gifts that honor his years of pipeline service.

Surprisingly, she longs for those simple newlywed days. Even though she used to get so mad that he always beat her in checkers or Wahoo, they had fun together. She even visited a toy store in pursuit of that same happiness, and returned with a Wahoo board.

While he no longer remembers his turn or can count the spaces, sometimes he still wins with her help. And she makes sure to celebrate.

That's the reality of Alzheimer's. She can fixate on the

losses or focus on days when the sparkle returns to his eyes (even just for a moment).

So on this day, she will wed. The hallway from her bathroom becomes an aisle they walk down hand in hand. Their secret ceremony is a reminder of the choice they've made each day - to love each other to the best of their abilities. She's thankful that's a part of the mind protected, for now.

Even if she has to become a bride daily, her answer will always be,

"Yes."

Ashlyn Parker is a small town author who specializes in journalism and children's stories. This is a true story dear to her heart. She hopes any readers touched by this testimony may consider donating to the Alzheimer Association in hopes of a future cure. You can follow Ashlyn's latest projects at @ashlynparkerauthor on Instagram

SAVING THE WATER AEROBICS CLASS

*Ben is back! Can he save the class,
GG, and his school-cool?*

Mevanee Parmer

My little brother Garrett sits on the porch, blubbering spit and tears. "Ca-Ca—Caleb next door says I'll never have a chicken show!"

"Well, I think you will! And I know you better'n he does. Shoot, you're smarter 'an he is and you're good with chickens!" I know these facts to be true. I put an arm around his heaving shoulders.

"Yeah, well I cain't get these chickens to do diddly-squat!"

"Listen, Garrett, my teacher says, 'Every challenge in life is like a little present wrapped with a great big bow. You just got to believe to achieve.' We'll show Caleb. He's a bully. If you want to take that Travellin' Chicken Show on the circus route, I'll help you get there."

Garrett looks up at me with wet cheeks. Slowly a grin spreads across his face, showing a space where a baby tooth had been. "Ben, you'll help me?"

"We can do this together, startin' this very afternoon, Little Buddy, sure 'nuff!"

Garrett is sure I can do anything, like train our chickens to walk across his flimsy rigged-up 2-by-4s, but I'm not sure about lots of other things. Like helping my great-grandma, GG, get to her water aerobics class.

My mom asks, "What can go wrong?"

Really? What if my friends find out? What if the cute Chewing Gum Girl who sits next to me in Shakespeare class sees me escorting GG and her walker into the Y? That will put a serious damper on my cool.

I follow Mom around the kitchen, "I cain't do this!"

She makes a quick turn, hands on her hips, "No whining, Ben! Of course you can. You've got your license now. I've taken you how many places over the last 16 years?"

I roll my eyes and sigh. *She has a point. I haven't always been as cool as I am today, and she took me everywhere with her when I was a dorky little kid.* I saunter over and lift the keys off the hall hooks. "Okay, but just this once."

"We shall see."

Yeah, I know. I'll be doing this on a regular basis.

"Oh, and you can't just sit there on your phone. Wear your swim trunks. You might have to jump in if you see GG's cute and darling curls going under." At 95, GG is the oldest active member at the Y, and she loves to tell everyone every time she gets a chance.

So here I am, swim trunks and tee-shirt, picking up GG, taking her to water aerobics. *Got this. Sittin' by the pool, cell phone for entertainment.*

I check her in and help her shuffle past the front desk. I duck my head and pull my baseball cap low over my face, but my six-feet-four-inch body is conspicuous. *I'll die if my friends see me here.* GG goes slow so she can be friendly, stopping to smile and say hello to people I know she cain't really see.

Mama's words echo in my head: "Gotta' have patience with Super Seniors." So I grit my teeth and keep a'shufflin'. Hours pass before we get down the hall, through the doors to the pool-side chairs.

Class is about to start, and I'm helping GG get in the water. There's her neighbor, Nana Guinn. She's waving like crazy.

Nana Guinn shouts, "I'm Ben's honorary Nana!"

Three more ladies start wavin' and shoutin', "I wanna be your Nana, too."

Epic! Guess I got my own Nana Group. I give them all imaginary high-fives.

Two teachers from school, Mr. and Mrs. Roberts, in their 60s, are the youngest people in the pool.

I'm finally in the clear when catastrophe strikes.

"Ben, it's you!" I freeze. *This jig is up. No chance of bein' cool-at-school now!*

Before I can turn around, a soft hand grabs my arm and guess what? It's a girl from my math class, Pony-Tail Talker. She's right up in my face! She's wearing a gray shirt with the Y logo and pink and white zebra-stripe exercise capris.

"You're so sweet! Is this your grandmother? She's been in this class forever."

"Well, she's my **great**-grandmother. We call her GG. Didn't know you were in this class," I duck my head. I can hardly look into her aqua blue eyes.

"Yeah, well, I teach this class. How great of you to be her escort, Ben."

How can I disappear into the concrete? She's patting me on the back and thinks I'm all humble about helping my sweet GG.

"Well, let me know if I can help you." I give her a wink.

She beams in my face, sincerely! This could be better than I ever imagined, a true midsummer night's dream. Suddenly my Super-Hero shirt is shining and I'm like the favorite person Pony-Tail Talker ever met.

I stride over to the patio furniture, glancing down into the pool.

At the far end, a 60-year-old lady wears a cowgirl hat, full Las Vegas-style make-up, and false eyelashes. She floats with a noodle wrapped around her back and her feet and legs propped up against the pool's edge.

"Hey, Cowboy."

Is she looking at me?

"How ya doin'?"

Too shocked to speak, I'm thinkin', *"Epic, lady, but you're older than my mother!"*

I sit down and pull out my phone just as Pony-Tail Talker announces, "Ladies and gentlemen, we have a guest teacher today. Ben's my friend, and he's offered to help out!"

What in the world! What's Pony-Tail Talker up to?

"Come on!" She waves me over. I put my phone under my cap on the patio table.

"Oh, no, really, I don't get wet too often, I mean like I do shower every day, I really .... But I don't get in a pool." *I'm a blubberin' idiot.*

"That's okay. I teach from the side! Not in the water," she whispers in my direction. She keeps pulling me over with that little come-here finger motion. She points to the empty space to her right. *Just for me?*

She shouts to the class, "Give Ben a big hand."

All the little ladies raise their hands over their heads in angelic applause. *Who can resist 24 sagging wings clapping?*

I stand beside Pony-Tail Talker to see what help she needs.

Vegas Cowgirl smiles broadly, "Now this class is better already."

Pony-Tail Talker starts the music with some songs from the '50s.

I expect a firm beat, not a lullaby. *What's up with "the doggie in the window. The one with the waggly tail"? What kind of lyrics are these? Cain't tell. Gotta focus on Pony-Tail Talker and her moves.*

"Barrel Jumping," she announces and jumps sideways, as if over a barrel. "Now the easier move is just slide sideways with no jump." She glides smoothly sidewise. "Ben, show us a good barrel jump."

I pretend to barrel jump as high as I can. The Nanas are

laughin'! *Ponytail, if I get too goofy, slip and knock myself out, will you give me mouth-to-mouth resuscitation? Will I remember it if you do?*

"Now cross the pool! We are walking BACKWARDS." So I do that, too, keeping about six feet from Pony-Tail. *I'd hate to trip over you, girl.*

Then I see him. I stop moving, and my jaw drops. The Casanova of the class appears and struts down the stairs into the water. All I can see is the tiniest skin-tight black swimsuit under a great big belly. Fluffy white hair encircles his head and covers his chest. His smile reveals two missing teeth. *Are you glarin' at me? Do you seriously think I'm competition?*

He shouts, "Hi, y'all."

He's wavin' at my Nanas!

I count four tattoos before he disappears into the water. His tooth to tattoo ratio is ominous. A few of the Nanas share a group groan in disgust. At the back of the pool, the Garden Party Gals giggle, jump up and down and give Casanova big waves. *He even has a following!*

Vegas Cowgirl sashays through the water toward him. "Well, hi there, Darlin'. You came just in time. Let's do a slow dance to this music."

Pony-Tail Talker keeps her cool. She shuffles up to me, turns me around, and gives me a nudge to get me walking backward again.

"Don't walk on tiptoes! Heels down, everyone!"

The class shouts back, "Ker Plunk!" laughing and splashing.

"March it out! Knees high!"

The class marches and chants in unison, "Woo-woo!"

Wow! They really have fun with this. I'm just barely keeping up when I see Casanova move his march next to my GG. *What are you thinkin'?*

He leans over and says something to GG I cain't hear. She probably cain't either. She never wears her hearing aids in the water.

Did you just say, "Hi, cutie!"? You'll look cute when I finish dunkin' you! Leave GG alone!

Pony-Tail Talker glances my way. I give her my "I'm bein' good" smile. *Did you notice I glared at Casanova? And that he glared back?*

"Next, Rocking Horse! Hands extended, leaning into your front leg. Hands pulled back, leaning on your back leg."

Did Pony-Tail explain it just for me? Oh no, do I look as dorky as I feel? I'm regressing!

Finally! I'm getting the hang of this. It's a challenge to follow and keep my eye on GG while Casanova has his eye on her, too. *How strange! I'm worryin' about romantic advances toward my 95-year-old GG. Is she worrying the same about me and Pony-Tail Talker? Man! Why cain't I remember her name?*

"Now Jumping Jacks!" Pony-Tail kicks up the pace into fast drive and suddenly slips, almost does the splits, and falls sidewise, her foot twisting under her. I rush to her side and help her up, but she's not putting any weight on her right foot. I pull over a patio chair, and she sits, rubbing her ankle.

"Keep going!" She grimaces at the class. "Get my phone, Ben. I gotta call the front desk." The Nanas stop and are staring, wide-eyed and open-mouthed. I can see Pony-Tail is really hurt and worried.

"Ben, take over for me. Just make up moves". I grab my phone, look for a 60s playlist, and plug it into the intercom.

Two burly guys arrive from down the hall and carry Pony-Tail perched on her chair through the doors and out of sight.

"Okay," my voice slides up an octave. I'm thinking of the old dance videos on YouTube. "Let's all do the Bangles' song 'Walk Like an Egyptian' back and forth." So I walk the walk, and the Nanas follow. Laughing, they hold their hands horizontal and poke in opposite directions.

"Next, let's do the Floss." I start the Floss, but they're all staring at me like I've lost my mind. *Where are you, Casanova? What! Beside GG! Too close, buster!*

"Okay, spread out and let's do the twist." That made them

happy. They all know the twist.

Casanova twists, still too close to GG. She looks up, shocked at Casanova and her head bobs barely above the water. Without thinking, I step to the edge of the pool, slip just before I dive, and summersault like a cannonball right into Casanova, who tries to catch me, but goes under. *Where am I? Landing on Casanova! At least I'm on top.*

He's all slippery skin, and I'm struggling to push off his hairy chest. *Are you trying to help me or drown me?* Frantic to get untangled, I shout as I break the surface, "I'm comin', GG!"

Before I can get there, Mrs. Roberts grabs GG. She pulls her up before her nose goes under.

GG is sputtering and coughing. I press heavily through the water over to GG and gently guide her to the stairs. Now her cute and darlin' white curls are damp. But she's chuckling and unhurt.

The class laughs and applauds! They think the front flip was on purpose! *Better than the* I Love Lucy *show.*

"Lead the class, Ben. I'm fine," GG shakes her head like a wet puppy. She sits on the top of the stairs, and I hurry back to leading class. Casanova climbs out, scowls at me, hands GG a towel, and thankfully heads toward the locker room.

We dance every move I ever heard of, including oldies like the Mashed Potato, the Watusi, and the Chicken Dance. Finally, the hour is done, the longest hour of my short life. The ladies all thank me for filling in. I make a theatrical, swooping bow.

Mrs. Roberts waddles her wet self carefully across the floor, "Ben, you did a good job teaching for Emmie."

Epic! Emmie! That's her name.

"You rose to the challenge," signaling thumbs up. I signal back.

Later that evening, I look up Emmie in our school directory and give her a call.

"Emmie, this is Ben. I—I just wanted to see if you're okay, you know, what with that epic fall in class." *Oh, No! That sounded bad.* "I mean, it was an athletic fall; you didn't mean to fall. Butuhh-are you okay now?"

"The doctor says I sprained my ankle." She sounds out of it, like someone on painkillers. "He says I have to stay off my foot for 2 whole weeks. Can you believe it?"

"Wow! I'm sorry. Can I bring you anything or do anything for you?" *Did I ask if I could do anything again? Where's my brain?*

"Well, that'd be sweet. Maybe bring me a chocolate shake from McDonald's—they're the best! And, ooh, would you mind subbing for me tomorrow at water class? Pleeease! That'd be awesome because you were doing great when I had to leave. Did class end okay?"

"Sure, everything was fine, more or less," I gulp, struggling to keep my voice even, "and I'd be happy to sub for you tomorrow. *What did I just say? I'm choking, fainting, watching myself do another front summersault into Casanova's arms. But I'm delivering the shake to her in person! All's well that ends well!*

"Oh, and I'm scheduled for **every** day for the next two weeks. So if you're not busy, just maybe, sub every day? The ladies do better if the teacher is someone they know. I could tell they think you're pretty cool."

"What? Okay, uh, maybe. When would you like me to bring your shake?" *Focus on the positive. Something good will come from this!*

"How about day-after-tomorrow in the afternoon? Three o'clock is good. Gus brought me one today, and Ryan is tomorrow. You're Friday?"

"Sure thing. *I'm your guy Friday!* I'll call and give ya' daily updates about the class if ya' like. Goodbye now." *Love's labor lost.* I flop on my bed. *At least I'll have a fan club of Nanas who think I'm cute. Casanova, don't mess with the best!*

Mevanee Parmer has returned physically and literarily to her roots in the Texas Panhandle, retiring after 23 years as a middle school teacher. She loves young adult fiction and especially the quirky perspectives of teenagers. She also has a passion for the voices of her High Plains ancestors. Her most recent publication, *Keep on the Sunny Side*, is a family memoir of faith and courage featuring over 100 vintage photographs, letters, and documents. She lives in Amarillo with her husband Phill Parmer and her aging mother, GG!

ROADSIDE CROSSES

Elise Phillips

When I was a kid, I had it all figured out. Become a journalist. Get a job with a Big, Important Newspaper. Win a Pulitzer. Become A Very Important Journalist. Get one of those late-night news talk shows. Be Rich.

Nowhere in that plan was there a trip to the top of Texas to search for a man named Tom. A man that could be anywhere on the maze of backroads within at least ten counties.

Needle. Haystack. Me.

Wouldn't my mom be proud. I thought of her as I drove the ruler-straight highway under the blindingly blue sky. I wondered what she was doing now. Probably still chain-smoking her way through the world. Tending bar in some dive. One of those places with a rifle under the bar. Stella Thomas-White wouldn't give a damn about my career failures. She'd only bum a twenty off me and then vanish again. Dear old mom hadn't spared much time for me in a decade. Not since I'd packed up my car and said I was moving to New York City to write for the Times. She'd laughed at me. So had the folks at the Times.

But, hey, at least I was living life on my own terms. If I'd followed Mom's lead, I would have ended up with a couple of kids from a couple of different guys. Probably. I'd probably be tending bar beside Mom, chain-smoking my way right behind her.

The Houston Chronicle wasn't the New York Times, but it was a great paper and I was happy for the steady job.

My big break was right around the corner. I hoped.

My first stop was the woman who had called the Chronicle with the story. I got lost twice before I found the little gray farmhouse in the middle of acres and acres of freshly plowed fields. It had rained the night before and the smell was intoxicating. Primal. I hadn't grown up around farming so it shouldn't have been so familiar, but it was. I just sat in my car with the window down and inhaled for a moment, letting it wash over me and fill me up. Petrichor. The smell of damp earth. Thank you, Word of the Day calendar.

"Can I help you?"

The shouted question broke the spell and reminded me that I had a job to do. It took two hours, a tour of the farm, and three glasses of iced tea to get the last known location of the mysterious Tom out of Mrs. Bell. It took a hand-drawn map and another hour before I found one of his crosses. Mrs. Bell had called them that—Tom's crosses. Grieving families put them up and Tom found them, repaired them, cared for them. And, according to Mrs. Bell, no one knew why. It was my job to answer that big question.

The cross was neat, tidy, and freshly painted. I could still smell the paint. The cross was simple, like dozens of others I'd seen in my life. A name was carefully painted on it - Diane - and a date. The weeds around it were neatly trimmed and a spray of plastic flowers was jammed into the ground before it. A simple memorial to someone who had lost their life on the lonely backroad. There was no sign of Tom. There were tire tracks in the mud, though. So I got back in my car and followed them.

"Good morning, Honey." I cringed and rolled my eyes. This is why I should look at the caller id before I answer the phone.

"Hi, Mom."

"Are you working? Am I bothering you?"

I sighed and looked across the gas station parking lot. I had been enjoying my convenience store breakfast before resuming my search for Tom. It was a pretty morning up here on the high plains. Still and peaceful - something that I rarely made time for back in Houston.

"I'm working but you're not bothering me. What's up?"

"I just wanted to check on you. It's been a while since we talked."

"I'm okay. On assignment up in the Panhandle chasing down some dude who cares for roadside crosses. You know, the ones families place at accident sites."

She was quiet for a moment. Mom was never quiet for a moment.

"Mom?"

"Your dad is one of those crosses, sweetie."

"Are you serious? You've never told me this."

"Oh of course I did. He was killed in an accident."

"That's all I know. Nothing else."

"He was up there in the Panhandle hauling cattle. Someone fell asleep and drove head on into him. They were both killed. His sister lived up there at the time. I know she put one of those crosses up for him. Maybe you'll find it. Look for two crosses together. Roy and, and...I think the other driver was a woman. Joan maybe."

Before I could ask any questions, I heard someone call her name and she was gone, ending the call without a goodbye. Typical. I wondered where she was. 7:30 in the morning was an odd time to be at a bar so she wasn't at work. Maybe meeting someone for breakfast or something. For all I knew she had a new job that wasn't in a bar. Maybe someday she'd stay on the phone long enough for me to ask. I tossed my phone on the dash and stood, staring at the road that disappeared into the prairie. I pictured a pair of white crosses on a lonely road, one bearing the name of the father I never knew, and wondered where they were and if Tom could take me to them.

◆ ◆ ◆

"I hear you're looking for me."

I looked up slowly, reluctant to abandon my game of solitaire, reluctant to talk to anyone after a long day of empty two-lane roads and fruitless searching.

"Excuse me?" I looked up at the man, taking him slowly. Dusty jeans, paint-splattered shirt, sweat-stained ball cap over bone-white hair. Three-day stubble on his sun-browned face. Gray-blue eyes glaring down at me. He pulled out the other chair, sat at my table, and stole a cold French fry off my plate.

"I hear you're looking for me."

"Are you Tom? The crosses man?"

"Yup. I know you or something?"

"You don't know me, sir, but I have been looking for you. I'm a journalist. I'd like to interview you about the crosses. I think there's a story in what you're doing that the world could use right now."

He leaned back in the chair, staring at me through narrowed eyes. I tried to read him but his face gave me nothing. Hardness was wrapped around him like a shield. I wondered if he used it to chase away people. It wasn't going to chase me off. That was one thing that made me really good at my job - it took a lot to chase me off. Those narrowed eyes and crossed arms clenched it for me. I would answer the unspoken challenge he was offering me. I would tell his story.

"No," he said, shoving away from the table and standing. As he walked to the door I threw a fist-full of cash on the table and grabbed my things. I was not going to lose this man again.

I caught him in the gravel parking lot. "Tom. Wait, please. Just talk to me for a minute. Hear me out." I skidded in front of him, slamming shut the driver's side door as I stopped my slide.

"Listen here, missy. I'm not buying what you're selling.

Leave me alone."

"I'm not selling anything, Tom. I'm just asking for a chance to tell your story. I think the idea of one person making the difference you're making is important."

"It's not making a difference. It's just…" He paused and his shield cracked a little. He looked past me to the open plains. "It's my penance."

"Let me ride with you. Share your story with me. I'll write it up. If you don't like it, I'll delete it and no one will ever know about it."

"No. This is about me. It doesn't affect the world at all. I don't make a bit of difference."

My turn to stop the conversation and look away. "It does make a difference, Tom. To me. I think my dad Roy's name is on one of the crosses you care for."

Tom stared hard like he saw me for the first time. Not an annoying stranger. Me.

"Get in," he finally said.

I was able to keep quiet for ten minutes before my reporter brain clicked on and questions started piling up inside my head. I was able to keep those from flooding out for another five minutes. I loved to ask questions so it was a personal best.

"Are you from this part of Texas, Tom?"

"Yes."

"Did you ever move away?"

"Yes."

"How long have you been working on the crosses?"

"A while."

I stopped and reassessed my approach. Tom was going to be a hard nut to crack.

"I grew up in the southern part of the state. Down by Beaumont. I've never spent much time in the Panhandle. It's beauty has surprised me. I like the openness. The emptiness."

He pointed across me, off to the west, toward a thunderstorm building on the horizon. "You see those clouds? They're not even in the state yet. They're over in New Mexico. Probably just east of Angel Fire."

"Really? I knew you could see far up here but I never thought about seeing into another state."

He nodded and focused on the road. "It's a hard place to love, the Panhandle. But to the people that do, there is no place like it. My family has been up here since the Comanches still ruled the area. None of us have ever been able to stay gone from it."

I waited, leaving him room to talk about whatever he needed to talk about.

"You know, most people don't pay any attention to those crosses. They're something you see everywhere, marking dangerous sections of roads all over the place. They're just something that's there, though. You never think about why they're there. At least I never did."

More questions flooded my mind and I fought to keep them tamped down. I wanted to know so much. Instead, I opened the notepad in my hand and started writing.

"Her name was Belle. I killed her six years ago when I was driving home drunk off my ass. Passed her and cut her off, clipping her front bumper. I was so drunk that I didn't know I'd done it until the sheriff came to my house. I served eleven months and then had to spend three months in a court-mandated treatment facility." He slowed down and flipped on his turn signal, guiding the truck onto a dirt road between two fields of corn. "When I got done with that, I had to see a shrink."

I wrote quickly, jotting down his words and adding the questions I was dying to ask. Hopefully I'd get the chance.

"I saw these damn crosses everywhere. Everywhere I drove. In spots I'd driven past all my life. They were haunting me. When I told my shrink, he gave me a job. Told me that maybe I was seeing the crosses for a reason. That I should take care of them." Tom paused and looked over at me for a second.

"So that's what I do now. I take care of them. People forget about them and they shouldn't."

I took my eyes off him for the first time when he started to slow the truck to a stop. I looked around and realized we'd left the corn behind and were back in open fields. The sun-bleached grass stretched away from us and in the distance I could see buildings and pens of cattle. My heart stopped and I looked to the side of the road.

Two crosses.

"You said your dad died up here. Roy, right."

"Yes," I whispered, slowly opening my door and slipping to the ground.

"I found these two about a year ago. Roy and Joanne. Was she riding with him?"

I walked toward the crosses and heard Tom's footsteps softly follow me.

"No. She killed him. She fell asleep and killed them both."

"These are some of the oldest ones I've found. I could barely read the names on them. I couldn't make out the dates."

I dropped to my knees in the soft dirt, unable to walk any closer. I looked up and down the road. It looked like a perfectly safe road. Straight as an arrow. No dips or rises. No sharp curves. People shouldn't die on safe roads like this.

"It was 1992. May of 1992. I hadn't even been born yet."

Tom walked past me with a small paint can and an artist's brush. As I watched, he knelt down, settled in front of the crosses and began to paint the date on each one.

"There we go," he said when he was finished. "Now people will know."

Tom walked back to me and offered me his hand. "Would you like to add the flowers?"

I took his hand and let him pull me to my feet. "I would, Tom. I really would."

◆ ◆ ◆

I rode with Tom for three days, picking pieces of his story out of our conversations about the weather, the crops, and the people in our lives. I told him about the father I'd never known and the three stepfathers who had come and gone in my life. He understood when I explained that my mother had eventually become the reckless older sister I had to rescue over and over. He'd had a younger brother who'd played a similar role in his life.

When he talked about the alcohol and the role addiction had played in his life, it was my turn to understand. My addiction had been a person, but his gravity had nearly made me throw away my whole life. We agreed that addiction was a devil with many faces.

At the end of the third day we had dinner in the diner where we'd first crossed paths. I asked him what he would do when winter settled over the Panhandle.

"I'm a carpenter by trade," he explained. "I'll spend the winter in my workshop. Build some furniture for friends and family. Take some odd jobs when they come my way. And I'll make crosses."

"Can you even put them up when the ground is frozen?"

"In my younger days, I would have had enough strength, but no, not anymore. There are some state troopers and deputy sheriffs who like to carry a cross or two in their cruisers. I make them for them."

"Do you ever think you'll be done with this, Tom?"

My question made him look away to the dark highway outside the diner windows. I looked there too, both of us watching as a truck pulled into the parking lot, filling the diner with a brief flash of yellow headlight beams.

No," he finally said. "No I won't. Hopefully someone will take over for me one day. Because you see, the thing is, you never stop needing crosses."

A fifth-generation Texan, Elise Phillips calls Amarillo home, where she resides with two weirdo pets. Currently working in marketing, Elise holds a Bachelor's degree in Agribusiness from West Texas A&M University and a Master's degree in English and Creative Writing from Southern New Hampshire University. Elise currently has three Christian Fiction novels out and is hard at work on a new Women's Fiction trilogy. In her free time, she not only writes but is also an artist and an occasional art teacher.

Her blog, art, and more can also be found on her Facebook page: https://www.facebook.com/writerelise.

THE PROBLEM OF SUFFERING

James D. Quiggle

A s a Christian, the subject matter for this year's anthology has led my mind to the problem of suffering. Most challenges involve suffering, in one way or another. My wife, for example, has continuing pain and difficulty walking, so, a physical challenge. Others suffer from mental, emotional, or spiritual challenges. I am, as a writer of Christian non-fiction (commentaries on Bible books and doctrine), an explainer, a sort of "technical writer" on the Scripture.

So when I think of challenges, I think of how the Scripture deals with the subject of suffering. This is an area of human experience the Bible speaks to. For example, the prophet Habakkuk wondered why God did not take action—why was God seemingly silent—when the wicked practice their wickedness and swallow the righteous (Habakkuk 1:13)?

This question has been used by skeptics in every age. Why doesn't God do something about suffering? How can God let that happen? My response is God has done something, but the world is not listening. Unless you possess omniscience, which you do not, you are not qualified to say whether or not God has intervened. Unless you possess holiness, who are you to judge

God? You, oh skeptic, are not qualified to act as God's judge.

God has done something. He has given his moral values and laws to humankind and expects humankind to practice those moral values and laws in every thought and every action. But humankind chooses to ignore God's morality. A recent in-the-news-example is pedophilia and child molestation. One of the states (California) in the United States has just passed legislation to keep certain pedophiles off the state's sexual offender registry, leaving it to the discretion of the judge.

So, asks the skeptic, where was God when this legislation was passed? Most nations, and most states, have laws against pedophilia and child molestation. Such actions are prosecuted when known, most often through a legal complaint. Why do those laws exist? Because God took action.

God has clearly stated his moral value concerning sexuality. Any form of sexuality is moral only as part of the marriage relationship between one male and one female and no other kind of relationship.

So, Mr. Skeptic, don't tell me God has not intervened if you have not taken action to live by and work justice according to God's moral values and commandments.

God will also intervene in the most absolute way. "The sexually immoral have their part in the lake which burns with fire and brimstone," Revelation 21:8.

The problem with the skeptic and atheist and secularist is they want God to intervene in every life but their own. Hypocrite! You are not willing God should intervene in your evil, but demand God stop the evil in others. If you reject God, and his moral values, and laws, and salvation, and judgment in your own life, then you don't have the moral standing to pass judgment upon God.

These same questions—Why is there suffering? Why doesn't God act?—have been echoed by the righteous in every age. But not as a complaint. Those with faith in God are seeking to understand what God is doing, and their part in God's works.

The biblical answers are directed toward those with

faith. The challenges God brings into a believer's life are intended to accomplish the following four general objectives.

For the believer to glorify God by persevering in the faith by faith. Christ never promised his saved people an easy life: "in the world you have affliction," John 16:33, because, John 15:19, "if you were of the world the world its own would love. But because you are not of the world . . . on account of this the world hates you." But Jesus Christ did promise to be with his people during all their life, good times and bad: "Never no never will I leave you, never no never will I forsake you," Hebrews 13:5. The believer's response to every challenge is, "My helper is the Lord, and I will not be afraid. What shall man do to me," Hebrews 13:6. That kind of response glorifies God, by recognizing God's works on behalf of the believer.

For the believer to be purged from indwelling sin and love of the world. The apostle John said (1 John 2:15), "Love not the world, nor the things in the world. If anyone habitually loves the world, the Father's love is not in him." The Lord's brother said, James 4:4, "Do you not know that the friendship of the Lord is enmity toward God." The believer is to "behave worthily of the Lord, pleasing in every way," Colossians 3:10.

For the believer to be purged of independence from God. A close examination of the life of Jesus Christ reveals the secret to a successful Christian manner of living: submission to and dependence upon God, even in challenging times, even during times of suffering. One example, in the Garden of Gethsemane, as he was suffering emotionally, Jesus called out in prayer, "My Father, if it is possible, let this cup pass from me. Nevertheless, not as I will, but as you," Matthew 26:39.

For the believer to testify of the grace and salvation of God. The apostle Paul said to the Philippians (4:13), "In everything I have strength in the one strengthening me." He had exampled that faith during his time in the Roman jail in the city of Philippi, Acts 16. He and his fellow missionary Silas sang and testified of God's grace and salvation in the jail cell, their feet bound in wooden stocks. When God sent an earthquake that freed them and other prisoners, the jailor, who had heard their testimony in songs and words, cried out, "Sirs, What must I do to be saved?" So also any Christian enduring the challenges of life may testify to the grace and salvation of God, by the manner in which he or she meets those challenges, by God's grace.

These are the reasons why believers suffer in the world.

Because life happens. The physical and moral laws of the universe are not suspended for the believer.

Because of circumstances. Believers suffer when the world they are in suffers. God makes his rain, fires, floods, and storms to fall on the just as well as the unjust. Believers endure and suffer with an attitude of joy whatever God brings upon the world.

Because of the world. This is by two means. One, by sin in the world sowing its seed and reaping its fruit. God allows sin to have its painful effect both as to punishment and natural consequences and as a goad to seek salvation in him alone. The ills of a sinful life testify to the sinner his/her alienation from God and only hope through faith in Christ the only Savior. Secondly, believers suffer from sinners directly attacking the believer for his or her faith.

To wean believers from the world. Whether one is newly saved or a maturing believer, the flesh is part of this world and struggles to remain at home in the world. The new believer must learn, grow, and mature in his or her faith to deny the world and the flesh. Misery in the world reveals to the believer this world is not home and has nothing to offer the godly soul.

To wean believers from their flesh. The nature of sin is rebellion against God: a selfish, self-centered autonomy. When faced with doubts and decisions, the first instinct, an instinct generated by the corruption of sin, is to rely upon self and not God. One sees the opposite in the mature believer. He/she will always turn to God for guidance, approval, and power. Misery in the world teaches the believer to live according to God's values, by God's spiritual empowerment.

To increase reliance and dependence on God. One effect of a trial is to replace dependence on the world and the flesh with dependence on God. This is how Jesus lived, with complete dependence and reliance upon God for all things in his life, including trials. This is how every believer should live.

To glorify God. Although believers suffer in common with the world, it is how they suffer, endure, and overcome that glorifies God. When the believer turns to God for guidance, approval, and power in times of trouble, he is not acting like the world; and, therefore, the weak human vessel is filled with the strength of God manifesting his glory to all creatures.

To draw sinners to saving faith. If in the suffering a believer glorifies God, then in that suffering, the Holy Spirit may use the believer to testify to the lost about the salvation found only through faith in God and God's testimony.

Believers suffer that they may not be condemned with the world. God addresses acts of sin committed by the believer in this life because for the believer, there is no sin, guilt of sin, or punishment for sin in the next life. Here and now, believers are plagued by an indwelling sin nature; they do suffer defeat by its temptations and do commit acts of sinning. God cannot have fellowship with sin. He chastises and cleanses the believer from acts of sinning so that fellowship may remain.

Believers suffer in order that unrepentant sinners may receive the greater punishment. This may be difficult to accept, but those who reject salvation continue in sin and reap to themselves judgment. Job 21:30, "For the wicked are reserved for the day of doom; they shall be brought out on the day of wrath." God is just in that the unrighteous, having chosen their lot in this present world, find their ful-fillment in this world and have no place in the world to come.

God uses the problems believers encounter in the world. Through them the believer may evaluate his or her faith; make a course-correction in one's manner of living; turn further away from sin; or act to mature one's faith. The believer should count it all joy that he or she is being weaned from the world and made fit for heavenly things, James 1:2 ff.

A final observation. We all battle with something debilitating, whether physical, mental, emotional, or spiritual. God so designed our nature that we do not succeed without challenges, that we must struggle and labor to be satisfied with our life. He also made us to help one another. So amazing then that we must begin our salvation with surrender to him, with submission to him, and live our salvation in dependence on him, even as we struggle and labor with the challenges he deliberately brings into our life so we can succeed in the life he gives us.

(All Scripture translations are the author's.)

FAILED JOURNEY TO FIJI

Janda Raker

It's been said that smooth trips do not make good travel stories. But challenging ones do!

As Lyle and I were planning our first big retirement trip--two-and-a-half months to New Zealand and Australia--we heard of a three-day bargain side trip to Fiji for only about $280 each. Wow! Of course, visions of beautiful beaches and palm trees surfaced, and we quickly signed on. But it turned out not quite as pictured.

That meager price included a resort hotel, with buffet meals three times a day. A few days lounging in Fiji seemed a perfect kickoff to our long sojourn. The only manageable time for our trip to Fiji would be Super Bowl weekend of 2000. So, we could watch the game at a beach bar with many other excited American tourists!

After flying from Amarillo to Los Angeles International Airport, we discovered the flight to Fiji was overbooked. The airline offered $800 each to wait for the next flight. Initially scheduled to board about 9:00 PM, we figured on a nap in the airport while waiting for the next flight. We signed forms, turned over our luggage, and asked the time of our new flight. Twenty-four hours later, the next night at 9:00 PM! What were we supposed to do in the meantime? Stay in a hotel with a cafeteria, at our own expense, just hang out in the airport, or take a bus into Los Angeles and shop. No! Excited to get out of the humdrum world of city life, to switch to tourist mode, we did not wish to include downtown L.A.

Lyle and I agreed to give up the $800 each, asked for our luggage back, tore up our agreements with the airline, and waited for our original boarding time, letting others have the $800.

The flight was difficult, the longest we had taken, about thirteen hours. We tried sleeping, but with little success. I stayed busy with the airline's magazine, crossword puzzle, my journal, and looking out into the ocean's darkness, watching for ships or islands with lights, but failed. And every hour or two, we walked through the plane's aisles, did stretches and squats, and drank water, while trying not to wake others more fortunate than we. Finally, many hours later, I was tired enough to sink into a deep sleep, only to wake in what seemed like only minutes later to the smell of bacon frying in the galley right behind us. Five AM, LA time. Rise and shine!

After breakfast, the passengers rose, bustled about, made trips to the toilet, requested juice to drink; babies cried, seniors coughed, and I never got back to sleep. When the plane finally reached the airport in Nadi, Fiji, on the west end of Viti Levu, the main island, both of us were exhausted. A slight black man in a tailored gabardine skirt and sandals held a cardboard sign with our last name. Though not talkative, he spoke a little British-sounding English—which turned out to be the lingua franca of the land. As he led us through the airport to a parking lot containing several vans and many small, elderly Japanese cars, he introduced himself—Harold.

In an ancient Toyota, he drove us northeastward, along winding streets, between coconut palms and fields of tall grass, from one village to another, some comprised of huts with thatched roofs. With gray peaks ahead and occasional glimpses of the Pacific, after perhaps thirty miles, finally he pulled into an attractive resort area, with white-painted archways, palm trees, birds calling through our open car windows, and broad welcoming driveways. Harold carried our backpacks to the registration desk. The clerk announced the evening meal would be served on the terrace in three hours. Harold took us and our packs to our room. All I saw was a cool, clean, dim space, with a comfy bed. I quickly peeled off my travel togs and hit the hay, with Lyle not far behind.

A few hours later, the sound of voices roused us, other tourists chatting as they walked toward the nearby terrace for supper. We pulled on shorts and sandals and headed off to join them.

After a scrumptious dinner, mostly seafood, fresh vegetables, and tasty desserts, we chatted with other visitors, twenty-five or thirty people from around the world. Lyle and I strolled down paved walkways between tiki torches, lush greenery, and attractive tropical sculptures, back to our room, finally taking time to admire the crisp, modern furnishings and a glass wall with a view of the dense forest past the foot of our bed, where we headed immediately.

Next morning, we were revived, enjoyed our breakfast of pastries and fruit, and took a walk around the facilities. Besides what we'd seen the night before, there was an exercise room and a gorgeous pool surrounded by tropical plants and vivid birds.

Soon we swam in the sparkling water and bright sunshine. Another couple was swimming, and we got acquainted. They were Brits, late fifties, likable. This was their first big trip without their kids, who were finally out on their own. But the last one, a daughter aged nineteen, was currently "missing in action." They hadn't heard from her in more than a month, despite their agreement that she call home once a week. She had chosen to drop out of university. She'd saved money from her first job, and then quit it to go off to New Zealand and stay with a friend she'd met at church camp. The parents knew it was illegal for her to work in New Zealand and also that she would definitely be out of money by that time. Terrified, they were barely able to enjoy their holiday, fearing what fate might have befallen her because she'd chosen not to call them to ask for money to return home. They knew her to be an intelligent, sensible young woman, but where was she? We commiserated, having raised strong-willed children of our own, but we could offer no real help.

Then Lyle thought to check on Super Bowl festivities for the next day. No signs posted announcements or times. And where was the beach? Photos of Fiji always include shots of tourists frolicking on the sand.

We strolled off the premises to see what the neighborhood was like and how far it was to the beach. Our resort nestled in a valley between verdant hillsides with coconut palms, lush ferns, and flowering shrubs. A one-lane gravel road wound out of the valley. Near the top of a hill, a tiny stucco building revealed itself to be a store, so we hiked up to the doorway. Padlocked shut! Bars blocked the front and side windows. But a deep, pleasant female voice behind the open front window asked, "You want to buy something?"

I approached, seeing that the bars slid to accommodate goods passed through. Not really shopping for certain items, we were just seeing what was available. Shelves lined the back wall, several feet behind the woman, who was only dimly visible, with long, dark hair and a patterned cotton top. I saw Cheerios, Twinkies, Ritz crackers, cans of Vienna sausages, canned chili, and less-identifiable products. Three people were approaching on the road, apparently locals, by their dress. Not wanting to cause the store to miss potential sales, I hurriedly ordered—Twinkies, for two, though not Lyle's favorite. And Cokes, of which she handed me two cans, lukewarm, without glasses or ice. She asked for 4.20 Fijian.

"How much in American money?" I queried, as we hadn't bothered to get any Fijian currency. She quoted the same price. I didn't know if that was logical or not, but I gave her a U.S. $5 bill, telling her to keep the change, which she happily did.

Ahead rose higher hills, forest, and narrow roads, without more buildings visible. So we headed back to our resort, partaking of our treats. In the hotel lobby, we stopped at the desk and asked the clerk where the beach was.

He said, "Not close."

I asked how far.

"A long drive."

"How long?"

"Many miles."

"How can we get there?"

"By taxi."

"When?"

"Tomorrow."

"Can we watch the Super Bowl here at the resort?"

"What is the Super Bowl?"

"American football. The championship, tomorrow. On TV."

The clerk looked puzzled. He pointed to a TV mounted high above a corner in the lobby. A game was being televised, which turned out to be Australian rules football. Lyle shook his head no.

The clerk said, "Not here. Maybe in the city of Suva."

Lyle said, "Where is Suva?"

"Many miles east."

Lyle asked how we could get there.

The clerk said, "By taxi."

A pattern had developed.

"Tomorrow?"

"Of course."

So we conferred for a minute, and then Lyle asked to have a cab waiting at 1:00 PM. Perhaps we wouldn't be watching the Super Bowl at a beach bar, but in a large, big-city hotel.

After our delicious evening meal of fresh fruit, baked fish fillets, vegetables, and non-iced tea, a four-piece band came to the little terrace and played oldies for our dancing pleasure. The Brits sat with us, and, between dances, we all talked of other trips we hoped to take and of the political mess created by the developed world, even in that year of 2000. And we got acquainted with several other guests--from Germany, Turkey, Hong Kong, India, and more. After cool beverages and light desserts, Lyle and I adjourned, looking forward to the next day's adventure.

After a croissant, a workout in the exercise room, and a shower, we donned fresh clothes to match the balmy weather and ate a light lunch. In the lobby, we met Harold, followed him to the parking area, and again boarded his auto.

He said, "To Suva, the city?"

I responded, "Can we go to the beach first?"

"The beach?"

"Yes, where people go to swim and ride in boats."

"Okaaay," he responded, somewhat hesitantly, and off we went.

He drove uphill, past the store, along the narrow road, finally joining a somewhat larger street—two lanes—with an occasional vehicle meeting us. The car wove in and out of woods and tiny villages, through a sleepy community, past maize fields and tobacco, across a narrow river, and to a small harbor where the river widened. Masts of compact sailboats rocked. Harold opened my car door, and we got out. Perhaps forty boats were visible, including about ten sailboats, twenty rowboats, a few minuscule open skiffs with decrepit outboard motors, and three larger antique sailing vessels, which were obviously being used as houseboats. At the edge of the dock, the view of the water included a sheen of oil glistening in the sunlight and globs of grunge and foam along the edges.

Harold looked at us, expectantly. "A beach?"

Did he not understand what we were looking for? We never knew. "Thanks. Very interesting. Let's go to the city," I proposed.

He seemed relieved, obviously comfortable with that request. We headed eastward—away from the river, with more curving roads, low mountain passes, to wider streets, and finally to highways congested with vehicles. Then Suva came into view. The downtown area had ornate buildings of British architecture mixed in with modern office buildings of six to eight stories. Harold asked where to go, but we didn't really know. Lyle suggested the largest hotel. Harold pulled up near a huge, elegant, tropical-style building across the boulevard from well-kept playing fields for rugby. We disembarked at the curb, busy with tourists, luggage, and cabs.

"What time shall I pick you up?" Harold asked.

With no idea what time the Super Bowl would start or end, Lyle shrugged. "Eight o'clock?"

We paid Harold for that leg of the trip and entered the cool lobby. The line at the front desk was short, and a large, dark desk clerk soon greeted us. "A room for tonight?"

"No," Lyle answered, "we want to watch the Super Bowl, and we thought the bar would host a watch party tonight."

"Super Bowl?"

My heart sank. He, too, didn't know what Lyle was talking about.

"American football. The championship," I said.

He shook his head. "We have TV in our bar with Australian rules football, but not American. The bar is there." He gestured. "You're welcome to go check."

The room was loud and dimly lit. The many TVs around the room all showed the same game. We spoke with the bartender, but no luck. I asked, "Would other hotels be showing the Super Bowl?"

"No. Not so many American tourists, and other countries don't care about American football." I felt deflated. But he was being honest.

Not to be deterred, Lyle and I walked north to the next hotel, a bright, modern facility across the street from Government Building Suva, the "capitol," with the same result. I had to admit I'd made a mistake, planning this part of the trip during Super Bowl week.

Roaming the hotel, we found a beautiful pool looking out over the Pacific, then located their mid-priced restaurant, and had a tasty meal of fish and chips with lukewarm tea. Back in the bar, we spent the next two hours watching and learning the sport of Australian rules football, which most fans call "footy." The room was crowded with tourists from many countries, though few were American. It was January, off-season for footy, and everyone was watching a rerun of the most recent championship playoff game from the previous September. Most were rooting for the North Melbourne Kangaroos.

The game was fascinating, with the players obviously much tougher than our NFL competitors--no padding to their uniforms, no helmets, and thirty-six players on the field at once. Lyle and I soon were cheering for the underdogs, the Carlton Blues, who finally lost, according to their complicated scoring system.

Afterward, we rushed out to the street just as Harold pulled up near the entrance of the hotel at exactly 8:00 PM, and we loaded into the back seat, hardly remembering that we had not accomplished our goals for that day or week—no beach, no Super Bowl. Our last night in Fiji ended with a late-night swim. We slept well, and next morning, Harold took us west, back to Nadi and the airport, rested and ready for our next adventure, heading for New Zealand and Australia.

Lyle and I were pleased with our trip to Fiji. Makes a good story. We never tried to find out where our resort was or the location of a beach from there. Later, I looked up the Super Bowl score: St. Louis Rams—23, Tennessee Titans—16, a great game. But we saw an excellent game too. And I would find the Brits' daughter in New Zealand!

So, it was a splendid trip after all, even with the challenges!

Janda Raker is an Amarillo native and award-winning travel writer and essayist who also writes profiles and short stories. Her travel articles have been published in Amarillo Style, UltraRunning, WingWorld, and others. She is now writing travel articles online for www.HubPages.com. She has published profiles in The Writer magazine. She edited and published two anthologies of very short stories with other authors--Flash Tales and Flash Tales 2. She is a retired educator with an MA in English and has critiqued and edited for many authors. She travels extensively, camping and enjoying nature as well as big cities around the world. Check her website, which includes links to her travel articles—www.TravelswithJanda.com.

SWEDISH GIRL POWWOWS WITH MOUNTAIN MEN

Betty M. Reeves

I n three weeks, Ulla Jonsson would return to Sweden. Before she would go, my family and I felt challenged to give this foreign exchange student an experience different from any other, an experience she would always remember. We took Ulla with us to a mountain man rendezvous.

Ulla came to the United States as an American Field Service (AFS) exchange student in July, 1979. She became the 'daughter' of Dan and Hazel Nelson of Dimmitt, Texas, and soon captured my heart as well as the hearts of most Dimmitt residents. My husband and I invited Ulla to attend the rendezvous with us and our two children.

The Sixth Annual National Rifle Association (NRA) Santa Fe Trail Rendezvous, in June, 1980, was just another event for many. For Ulla, it was packed with exciting, first-time experiences. The rendezvous was and continues to be a gathering time for mountain men, buckskinners, muzzleloaders, and their families. The original rendezvouses of the 1800s were located at remote meeting sites and allowed mountain men to meet and sell furs or make trades for other items.

Ulla was impressed with the deep canyons and rugged

ridges of the NRA Whittington Center near Raton, New Mexico. These foothills to the expansive Rocky Mountains were different from any place Ulla had been.

Our primitive camping was not unknown to Ulla, a long-time Swedish Scout. She helped us set up our 'special tent' under the lone shade tree in that part of Coal Canyon. Automobiles were not allowed past a certain, marked point unless loading or unloading, but all camping and parking areas were well within walking distance of the black-powder target ranges and Tipi Village.

Ulla's questions, comments, and openness with the mountain men and their families soon endeared her to them. They were always very receptive to her bubbly personality. She was eager to learn all she could from her new friends.

Her being a foreigner helped keep the mountain men patient and willing to answer in detail Ulla's numerous questions and puzzled looks. They made great efforts to explain their lifestyle, as they would to any interested outsider.

Even though we told Ulla what to expect, she seemed awed by the rough appearances of many buckskinners in their true frontier garb. She was impressed upon learning that the costumes were handmade in the clothing styles of American pioneer trappers.

Ulla was more interested in Tipi Village than in anything else. She learned that not all North American natives lived in tipis, that tipis are not round at the base but egg-shaped, and that tipis are cooler in summer and warmer in winter than modern tents. She even sat in the grass and studied the setting-up of a tipi, from its being unloaded to the building of a campfire in its center.

Later, the 18-year-old Swede watched as the trappers arranged their trade blankets. The blankets were covered with beadwork, pouches, pipes, skins, and other wares.

Ulla soon became accustomed to the "booms" of black-powder shooting events and to the informal, unstructured ways of the participants. With coaching, Ulla became quite good in tomahawk throwing events. Hoorays and whoops rose from the onlookers each time the robust girl hit her mark.

The true meaning of the council fire powwows and the smoking of the pipe rituals were never clear to Ulla. However, she thought they were beautiful ceremonies.

A young couple chose to be married during the rendez-vous. Ulla found the authentic buckskinners' wedding to be the most moving and lovely event of the four-day weekend. Two bagpipers in full regalia led the wedding march along with buckskinner 'McTavish' from Albuquerque, New Mexico.

Next in the procession were the groom John Torrance, dressed in buckskins and a red flannel shirt, and his bride Fran, in a black wool dress trimmed with red. They were followed by their friends from Missouri and Ulla.

The wedding party circled inside Tipi Village and stopped before the tipi of 'Crow Caller' and 'Delicate Flower.' The ensuing Native American ceremony was performed by a local minister who had arrived wearing a typical suit and tie. He had quickly been re-adorned in mountain-man garb.

The ceremony included tributes to the newlyweds and the naming of the couple. John was to be called 'Hunter of Small Buffalo (beaver),' and Fran was given the name of 'Shining Meadows.' Ulla offered heartfelt congratulations to the couple, and we presented them with our gifts of home-dried peaches and a bead necklace.

To show his total acceptance of Ulla, Bub 'Skin Head' Ady presented a badger claw to Ulla. She understood this act of friendship after he explained that the badger was his totem. He said that a totem, often an animal, represents an individual and traits of that individual. "You don't choose a totem," he added, "Your totem chooses you."

'Skin Head' and other mountain men killed rattlesnakes and cooked the meat. Though skeptical at first, Ulla tried her serving. The cooks waited expectantly for her reaction.

"It's good!" Ulla exclaimed, adding, "It tastes like tough chicken." Also for the first time, Ulla ate horse jerky and calf fries. She really liked the calf fries.

I knew that our challenge to give Ulla a singular experience was accomplished when she said, "I don't know how to explain all of this to my Swedish family."

One evening, a curious bear strolled down from the mountains to see what was happening. Several buckskinners were able to walk within 50 yards of the blond-colored bear before it climbed a tree. Ulla snapped several pictures of the friendly critter, from a very safe distance, of course. This was the second year that the same bear visited the rendezvous.

One morning, Ulla carried water about a half-mile from the water truck to our tent. She sponge bathed and washed her hair. Then, we walked to Tipi Village.

A mountain man turned and asked, "Who smells so good?"

"It must be Ulla," I said, "She's clean."

"That's disgusting," he joked.

The liars' contests? Well, they were something else! Ulla would listen intently, then she would shake her head in dismay.

'Skin Head' asked, "Ulla, do you think all of us are weird?"

"You're not weird," Ulla announced, "You're DIFFERENT!"

Ulla was beginning to understand that the people who frequent the mountain-man gatherings are unique. Since the early 1800s, mountain men have been unable to explain their lifestyle to society. Perhaps words will never be adequate. Perhaps most of their contemporaries will never understand them.

Ulla grasped the idea that these men and their families choose an alternate way of life, even if for limited times, to be in harmony with nature and with each other. Yes, they certainly are DIFFERENT.

Bub 'Skin Head' Ady cooked rattlesnake.

Ulla Jonsson tasted the cooked rattlesnake.

Betty M Reeves has written two music books, Melody Street: Story and Illustrations and Guitars & Folk Songs: An Anthology. With daughter Elayne M Hoover-Sims, Betty co-authored The Story of Glops, a Christian book for kids. Betty has continued telling about glops in a Christian historical fiction series. She is an arranger, composer, and self-publisher. She taught music for 23 years and volunteers in the music ministry of her church. She holds a Bachelor of Music Education from Texas Tech University and a Master of Arts in Music with Kodaly Certification from WTA&M University. Betty and her husband Glenn live in Borger and Amarillo, Texas. They are blessed with five grown children, nine grandchildren, and many great-grandchildren.

IT IS GOING TO BE OKAY

Lou Sheldon

"It is going to be okay," the Pastor said. He was holding my hand, reassuring me. I could not open my eyes to look at him, but I knew he was there. I did not know where we were exactly, except that it was quiet, very quiet. I drew strength from his voice as he kept repeating the same phrase, over and over, "It is going to be okay."

Without warning, the peaceful, strengthening feeling was jerked away. I found myself gasping for air and retching as I lay on some kind of hard table. A pungent, danger smell was in the air, and I shivered from the cold. Soft hands moved over my body, helping me to turn to the side. I could hear urgent voices yelling things back and forth, but I could not follow what they were saying; my mind was numb. A face flashed above me, but the person disappeared as quickly as they had come.

I shuddered as the table I was on collided with something and then the wail of sirens competed with more strident voices. I cried inside of myself, God, where are you? Help me! I was afraid and wondered where the hand of the Pastor was, wishing he was with me. Within moments, everything slowed down and I felt myself drifting far away from all of the noise and confusion. A dark void drew me in and I went to it, hoping I would find the Pastor there.

Where am I? What is happening? My mind struggled to make sense of everything. I knew I was not on the hard table anymore. Instead, I was lying on something comfortable, and I was cozy and warm. The urgent voices were gone, and rhythmic, swishing noises came and went to my side. My scratchy socks bothered me but I did not have the strength to remove them. I tried to force my eyes open a crack to get my bearings but realized the effort was not worth it. I returned to the relief of the blackness.

Hands were prodding me. Not the soft hands from before, but hands that were strong and assertive. "Stop it!" I cried, blinking my eyes several times in an attempt to see who was pulling at me. My head swam as I tried to sit up. "Well, I guess she is feeling better. That is a good sign," a deep voice said. Someone in white was standing next to me and continued touching my body in rough ways. What is he doing? Leave me alone!

As I struggled to become alert, my senses felt overwhelmed with all the noises and smells engulfing me. Beeping machines, squeaky shoes, ringing phones, laughter, and carts rolling by mixed together and filled my ears until my head pounded. My stomach began to roll as sharp chemical smells, woodsy aftershave, and flowery perfume lay heavy around me.

Pain shot through me several times as I was pushed this way and that. I cried out but the person in white kept on going, torturing me. Help me! Someone make him stop! I sensed another presence next to the person hurting me, and then my mind started to become fuzzy again. Was it the Pastor? Was he making the aggressive person stop his assault? Before I could think about it anymore, I detected a dimness approaching and welcomed it.

I heard them before I saw them. I lay on what I assumed was a bed and listened in on their conversation. A thick gravelly voice that was not happy blended with a light musical voice that sounded scared. "She was lucky. She got the worst of it. It was very difficult to get her out of the car. Frankly, I don't know how she survived. The rest of the kids were fine. A bit shook up, but fine. The other driver was drunk. Stupid idiot!"

"Thank you, doctor." Hey, I know that voice. That is my older sister. What is she doing here? I felt her hand grasp my own, and it was trembling. I willed my eyelids open and searched for her face. She saw the movement and leaned over, smiling, and touched the side of my cheek. "Hey sweetie, you are going to be okay. Mom sent me down to check on you since she does not drive. You sure gave us all a scare."

My body ached all over, but her hand in mine seemed to help the pain diminish a bit. It was not the same as when the Pastor held my hand, but her closeness was so nice. I gave her hand a light squeeze and tried to smile back at her. I wanted to talk to her but my mouth was full of cotton and I could not make my tongue work right. I gave up and closed my eyes. I was so, so tired. I would have to wait until later to ask her my questions.

My sister took me home after I was released from the hospital. I had been at a church youth group dance a few towns over from my own with some friends. Evidently, a drunk driver had smashed into us as we drove home. I asked my sister to take me to see my mangled car but she would not hear of it. It was my very first car, and I was so proud of it even though it was an older, used car my brother got somewhere. Having my own vehicle allowed me to get good jobs across town from where we lived. I did not know what life would be like without it.

As my sister and I drove home, I tried to make sense of everything. I recalled being at the dance, having a good time with my friends, and part of the drive home in my car as we laughed and enjoyed ourselves. I did not remember the crash itself, but the memory of the Pastor holding my hand was so tangible. My body was sore, but thankfully I did not have any broken bones or other substantial injuries. The doctor said the nasty looking bruising would eventually go away. I was to rest and not push myself and gradually ease back into things.

My Mom and friends were waiting for us at the front door of our house. Mom had tears in her eyes. She hugged me, and we all went into the kitchen and sat around our big table, eager to talk and reconnect. My story came out in bits and pieces as I tried to relay what I remembered. For some reason, I did not mention the Pastor right away. I felt funny talking about him, like it was a private moment I wanted to keep to myself. My sister filled everyone in on what the hospital staff said about how lucky I was to be alive. I did not realize until that moment, the emergency crew thought they had lost me for quite a while after pulling me from the wreckage.

Mom turned white as my sister talked, and then Mom whispered in a shaky voice, "It is God's mercy." Her voice strengthened as she continued, "He woke me up to pray for you long before I got the phone call from the police that you were in an accident. I remembered Pastor Pete teaching about Psalm 91 being a prayer of protection, so I prayed it over you. I did not know what was wrong, just that you were in danger."

At the mention of Pastor Pete, I clasped my hands tightly together under the kitchen table and waited for Mom to finish. I was now eager to finally share with someone about what had happened. "He was there, Mom. Pastor Pete was there with me after the accident. I felt him holding my hand. He kept saying that it was going to be okay." There, I had finally told someone. It sounded crazy. How could he be there with me?

Mom began to cry again. "Yes, that makes sense. He would be the one that God would send to be with you. He helped you grow so much in your faith after you became a Christian." What no one had to say was that Pastor Pete died a few months previous and had been a tremendous blessing to our family the last few years.

"God knew exactly who to send to be with you, little one. It had to be someone you would trust and would encourage you to hold on and believe that things would be okay. Thank God for His mercy and His angels watching over you."

For several moments we all sat in silence around the table, our thoughts full of Pastor Pete and his many kindnesses, what could have happened and the nearness of God in our everyday lives. The rich smell of brewing coffee filled the room and helped us break free from our reverie. Mom went for coffee cups and I jumped up to get some snacks out for our guests. Today was a celebration day and it felt good to have friends and family to share it with.

*Many of the people who sat with me around our big kitchen table those many years ago have passed on. Only a few remain who remember the night God performed a miracle for a high school kid still wet behind the ears. Even though it has been decades ago, the event is still as real to me today as the night danger almost swallowed me up. Sometimes, especially during difficult times, the words heaven sent through Pastor Pete of, "It is going to be okay," still echo in my soul. Combined with the Word of God and prayer, those significant words produce a strength that carries me forward to face the challenges of the day.

Over the years, I have learned that things 'being okay' does not necessarily mean life will be easy. Rather, that God will walk with us through the hard times we encounter. I will always be thankful for His intervention that night many years ago, as well as for a mother who was obedient to pray for one of her children in a time of need. I am glad she did not decide to roll over and go back to sleep instead that fateful night or she would never have met her beautiful granddaughter, who is so much like her.

OLD FISHING RODS
WANTED

Lou Sheldon

My friends sometimes ask why I keep old fishing rods in my shed. Such a question always leads into telling them about my Daddy. Daddy fished with his father during the Great Depression as a way to help feed their good-sized family. They fished from the bank and also made fishing traps that they set and later checked on. The duo spent hours in the countryside, working side by side to get a good haul. Daddy told me during one of our last conversations before he passed on that some of the best memories from his childhood were the moments he spent fishing with his father.

Daddy never mentioned if the weather was warm or cold while fishing with my grandfather. That did not seem to matter, even though South Dakota can be quite chilly from fall to late spring. I have seen it snow into May there before, so I can imagine the cold probably left them exhausted at times. Daddy only spoke of how strong his father was and what a hard worker he was. Maybe that is why my Daddy was such a hard worker. Perhaps he wanted to be like his own father as a way to remember him.

You see, my grandfather was not around very much while

my Daddy was growing up. Grandfather went away during the Great Depression and left Daddy, who was just a youth, in charge of taking care of his brother and sisters and mother. It was a very difficult season in Daddy's life, and they all ended up living out of the family car, parked next to a river, for a while. It was a safe place and provided a source of food for them. Only because of the goodness of the Catholic nuns in town did their family make it through that period successfully.

Years later, when us kids and Mama went fishing with Daddy, it was like a secret part of him was allowed to come out to play. During the work week, Daddy usually got pretty weary and cranky. I grew up staying out of his way on his tired days, but I always looked forward to him being relaxed on family fishing trips. When we all climbed into our station wagon and headed to one of Daddy's favorite fishing spots, the air in the vehicle was electric with excitement.

On the car ride there, my brothers loved to squabble over who had the biggest nightcrawlers and who would bring in the first fish. As we bumped along, my older sisters tried to out-sing each other with the latest teen love songs, all the time wondering if any boys would be fishing in the vicinity of where we would be at. Even us younger kids got caught up in the fun, thinking of the rocks and shells we would collect and take home to show our friends and grandparents.

Once we arrived at the fishing hole, Daddy was extra gentle with us little kids while he set our lines for us. He made sure that we were close to where he and Mama staked out a little area for themselves along the bank. That way, they were handy in case we needed them and where he could keep watch over our lines. All day, Daddy's eyes twinkled while we fished, ate our packed lunch, and fished some more. It made my heart so warm when Daddy turned those twinkling eyes on me in his tranquil mood. As I explored up and down the bank, visiting my brothers and sisters fishing lines, I could hear Daddy's rich laughter. I drew that laughter deep into myself to be remembered during the tired times when the crabby side of Daddy erupted during the work week.

By late afternoon, Mama and Daddy had the job of rounding up a bunch of tired and dirty kids and squeezing us all back into our car for the ride home. Somehow, the station wagon always felt smaller on the return trip with it full of wet gear and bags of collectibles. Most times our coolers were packed to the rim with the catch of the day, and we all looked forward to a meal of fried fish that we had caught ourselves. A fishy odor permeated the vehicle, but to me it was a special perfume signaling time spent together as a family.

As dusk settled in and the headlights of other cars flicked on around us, my siblings and I struggled to not fall fully asleep, drawing our windbreakers over ourselves for covers. Big and small alike, we leaned our heads on each other for support. Bouncing down country roads, we whispered back and forth about the day's adventures. In the front seat, the glow from the dashboard illuminated Mama and Daddy as they spoke in low tones and exchanged a laugh now and then. Daddy's metal thermos sat between them in the little snack box that held the wet washcloths packed in plastic baggies that Mama always brought along on trips. Every once in a while, Mama would refill Daddy's coffee mug for him or adjust the radio to the next country music station.

All us kids knew not to let our eyes close too much in case Daddy topped off the day with a surprise visit to an A & W Root beer stand. The older kids helped watch for signs along the road directing travelers to such a heavenly place. Daddy had a sweet tooth, so we knew there was always a good chance of such a treat. If and when we finally did pull into an A & W to order our root beer floats, it was hard to think about the work week ahead and the worn-out Daddy that we might encounter.

Over the years, my siblings and I may not have always understood or valued the drive and determination of our Daddy, but his love of fishing is one quality I will always appreciate about him. My Daddy was a different person when he gathered his gear and headed for a good fishing hole. God worked through the healing found in nature and the memories evoked while fishing to help Daddy. It was there while listening to wild bird calls, smelling the pungent fishing bank, and feeling the sun on our faces that Daddy tapped into a reservoir of love within himself that he could share with Mama and us kids.

The moments I shared with Mama, Daddy, and my brothers and sisters while fishing are a treasured part of who I am. For that reason, old fishing rods that I have collected over the years will always have a home in my shed or until someone else can use them to create new memories. Either way, whether they stay or go to someone else's home, the old rods are a loving tribute to my Daddy, a man who passed on the gift of fishing together as a way to say he cared for and loved his family.

HUNGER

Coby C. Spurrier

I saw the gold, and I took it. A different man might not have, I know that, and from time to time, I think back on the hour when I saw the gold and took it. You see, I was hungry. Isn't it ironic?

I don't remember much else about that night but the gold and the hunger. I don't remember the name of the tavern or even the village, but it was somewhere in southern Iiauskana. I can't really be certain. For some time, I sat dumbly in my chair, my mind occupied with nothing but the pain in my stomach. If you've never been truly hungry from days of no food, you can't know what it's like. You can't concentrate on anything. It wasn't until a figure to my left got up from the table to get a drink and left a stack of gold madas behind that I snapped to awareness.

From this moment on, my memory is crystal clear.

My eyes to the gold. My eyes to the stranger's back, walking calmly toward the barmaid. My hand to the gold. The gold in my pocket. I'm up from the table and out the door. For just a moment, I look back. The stranger has turned to look my way. He wears a hood, but I can feel his eyes meet mine. I swear, I can sense a slight smile.

Out into the street, and behind some barrels, I crouched down, waiting for my pursuer. One benefit of a lifetime running from guards, I know how to disappear. For nearly an hour, I waited there, suffering even more from hunger. You see, I was awake now and I had the means to buy myself a feast. This knowledge tortured me. When I finally got to my feet, I very nearly fainted. I had only enough energy to walk to the other edge of the village to a run-down tavern before collapsing at a table. I think I must have fallen unconscious for a moment before I heard the barmaid's voice.

"Can I get you something to eat, sir?"

I gorged myself on roasts and pies and huge overfilling mugs of elven ale. As the fog of near-fatal starvation began to lift, I looked up from my plate to see a gold-masked stranger looking at me, his vizard glowing by the blinding light of the moon through the window. He wore black leather armor and was a different physique and size from the man I had burgled, but I could tell he knew. I paid for my meal quickly and left.

I skirted the edge of the village, through a tiled central courtyard surrounded by the squalid peasant's cottages. There was not a light shining from any window or door. No one was on the streets. I could find no place to hide, so I took the road out of town, heading for the wilderness. Hunger had pushed me on in the days before, but now I felt what I imagined to be the whip of guilt. Or perhaps, even then, it was fear.

I fell twice, rushing down the dark path, unused to the slopes and pebbled texture. The sounds of animal life, which I had numbed to, were suddenly very loud in my ears. And there was something else out there in the night, something chasing me.

On the side of the road, there was a low wall, and I scrambled over it and hid. I knew enough about concealment to pick a spot where the wall sunk slightly, so even if someone saw the outline of my figure, he would assume it to be part of the wall. It wasn't long before I heard the sound of running footsteps from more than one person pass me by and then stop. There was a moment of whispered conversation, and one of the people ran back on the path toward the village. Then, silence.

After a few more minutes, I peered out from behind the wall. A female figure in a dun gown, wimple, and veil stood in the road. On the other end of the road, blocking the way back to town, was a knight, coated in dark mail. I could see neither of their faces. For a moment, I froze, unsure whether either or both had seen me.

"Run," said the woman in a dead voice.

The hill behind me was too steep, so I leapt over the wall and across the road in two bounds. Into the night forest I ran, the maddening jingle of the accursed gold in my pocket. I knew I was making so much noise my pursuers could not help but hear me, but now I cared more for putting distance between us than in stealth. Clouds filtered through the moonlight, but I still knew it was too bright to hide. I ran and ran until I felt all my blood pumping in my head and heart, begging me to stop.

I was at the edge of the wood, on the other side of a shallow stream from a vast, crumbling house encircled by a rail fence. Behind me, running footfall in the broken, dusty earth. To the south, downstream, a distinct sodden splashing of someone moving nearer.

There was no choice. I half jumped and half fell into the mud and dragged myself up the bank on the other side. I rolled under the fence and ran through the open field toward the house. Jerking my head around, I saw seven shadowy figures by the fence posts. The cloaked man I had robbed. The man in the gold mask. The veiled woman. The dark knight. Three others too who had pursued me, but I had never seen. And I thought I was the stealthy one.

The moon was entirely hidden in a swarm of cloud. Only the stars offered their meager illumination as I reached the open door of the ruin. I slammed and bolted the door behind me, but I knew there could be no protection for exceedingly long. As I looked about the ravaged interior of broken furniture, I searched for somewhere to hide. A corner, where if I stayed very still, no one would see me.

A splintered table lying against the wall looked perfect

for my purposes. I crawled under it and jumped when something moved, and I heard a frightened old man's voice.

"Who's there?"

"It's all right," I whispered. "I'm not one of them."

His puckered, gnarled hand reached out from the shadow and gripped my arm. Instantly, I felt sleep fall upon me, resist it as I might. The old man's horrible face, the face of the hungry dead, emerged as the moon came out and shone through the broken window. His talon still gripping me, I fell back, smelling his death surround me.

The table was thrown back. There stood the seven hunters and a dozen more. No, hunters they weren't. They were harriers who had chased me out of every hiding place, expertly pushing me to the lair of the real predator. He was weak with age; the old man was not as good at the chase as once he was. A blunt, killing machine.

"Please," I said. It was all I could muster.

Having enjoyed the sport I offered, he granted me mercy, of sorts. I was not bled dry. I was not cursed by being made one of them, the Berne. I was kept with others, most of us mad with fear, to be aged and tasted at the vampires' whim. We are called cattle.

I lost all hope months ago of ever leaving the dank cellar where they keep us. Even if this note finds its way to the outside world, I cannot give enough information about my whereabouts to be rescued, even if some champion were able to defeat the bloodsuckers. I only write this to keep my own sanity and to warn others.

There is something worse than being hungry.

Being...food.

Coby Chase Spurrier is a young autistic gamer, writer, and worldbuilder. He currently lives in Amarillo, Texas, with his dad. Coby works part-time at MarketStreet United while he finishes his books in fantasy and Syfy.

THE LAST GASP

Rick Treon

I asked for this. For the prairie grass scratching at my upper ankles, evading the sneakers and socks. For the sound of snakes and other creatures rustling through that grass as I slog toward an old abandoned farmhouse.

For the task of making sure a squatter doesn't live here. Or, worse, an isolationist who'd rather spend money on drugs and drink than home repairs and landscaping.

I met him a week ago, a manic skeleton who threatened to sic his dog on me. The large black Chow looked friendly enough until hearing from its master. In the end, he provided the one answer I truly needed before I backed off his property.

These are the kinds of challenging cases I requested. And why wouldn't I? More hours. More mileage. More money.

So I creep closer to the house, a graying wooden home still surrounded by evergreens to break the Texas Panhandle wind.

I intend to knock on the door and ensure nobody's home to interview, but the sound comes before I reach the door—a million insects at work. And not the crickets I'm used to hearing near dusk in fields northeast of Amarillo and southwest of nowhere, but flies, orbiting the poor antelope that couldn't find its way out.

I might've left then, marked the house abandoned and called it a night. But as I turn, my brain finally isolates the stench, now unmistakable as it is foul.

◆ ◆ ◆

I did not ask for this. Not the talking to the sheriff's deputy. Not the late-summer insects feasting on my shins as the sun falls victim to a flat horizon.

And certainly not the body rolling past me.

Though macabre, I wonder whether I'm still on the clock. I pull out my work cell—a government-issued iPhone with a Dallas area code and internet restrictions—and text my supervisor.

Still here. Waiting for the investigator. How do I handle my timesheet?

If standing near a possible crime scene didn't count as work, I'd miss out on an hour's overtime. Only thirty-five bucks, but I need every dime of it.

Three dots are still dancing on the screen when Matthew McConoughey yips my first name.

I looked up to find a man, older and much heavier than the actor, gingerly crossing a nearby cattle guard.

"So, you're the lucky lady who found the DB," he says, not bothering to translate the cop jargon despite the fact I'm now a civilian.

I nod. "Yessir. I'm working for ..."

"I've been briefed, Mrs. Reynolds."

I'm not sure what my face does upon hearing that name, but it must adequately convey my mixture of confusion and disgust.

"Oh, that's right. My condolences on the divorce. Got one of those myself, though that was a long time ago now."

This man, who I can only assume is a Texas Ranger, is talking as though we were old friends.

"I'm sorry," I ask, trying my best not to sound discourteous, "but do we know each other?"

He continues his slow but steady march toward me before stopping about ten yards away. "Now that you mention it, I don't think we ever met in person, just on a conference call. I'm Lieutenant William Cody. But most people call me—"

"Buffalo Bill."

I maintain control over my facial muscles, but he doesn't need a visible reaction to smile at my embarrassment. The last time I worked with the Rangers, I called Lt. Cody something I hope never to repeat.

I was off the force a few months later. My outburst wasn't the reason, though it surely didn't help.

"So it's back to Lori Young, then?"

I nod.

"Well, Ms. Young, I have to wonder about the odds of a former Amarillo homicide detective catching a case in the middle of nowhere nearly two hours from home."

"They're probably the same as a man named William Cody owning a ranch with a herd of bison."

This time his smile is friendly. "You'll understand if we get your prints and a swab to rule you out."

I motion to the CSI van, now occupied by the body. "They have everything in there? Or will I have to drive to Dumas?"

"We can take care of it here. Shouldn't take long." He steps closer, and I am careful not to edge backward. "While we wait, can I get some proof that you were here on official business?"

I pull out the work cell—a green banner informs me that no, I am not getting paid to talk with Buffalo Bill—and open the government app. After navigating to a GPS map, I close the distance between us and zoom in on our location.

"The blue dot is us," I say, "and the blue pin is the house." I tap on the icon and it pulls up the address, though it only gives the farm-to-market road and a descriptor: OLD WOOD HSE LRG WNDWS.

"All right then, I'll round up the techs so we can get you home at a decent hour." He whistles using his thumb and index finger, then waves one of the men in white jumpsuits our way.

I have one final ask. As we begin the trek toward our respective pickups, I insert myself into the case despite having been stripped of any right to professional courtesy.

"Any idea who he was?"

He's silent for a few steps while considering my inquiry. A nod finally lets me know whatever he's heard about my abrupt dismissal from the APD isn't enough to keep him from humoring me.

"Won't get a positive ID for a bit, but all indications are he's the man wanted for robbing that Allsup's in Stinnett."

I take a moment to recall the case. "He and the clerk opened fire on each other, right?"

"Right," he says, motioning me to continue toward our vehicles on the other side of the cattle guard. "Third time this year after the state started encouraging armed cashiers. Anyway, our guy was hit but still managed to haul hind tail north on 136. Locals found the old Firebird he was driving abandoned in a cornfield. There was plenty of blood inside, but dogs lost the scent a mile or so out."

I laugh as we approach our respective pickups during twilight's last gasp. "Wonder if I still get to collect the store's reward money. I don't remember the wanted poster saying dead or alive."

Buffalo Bill shakes his head. "You'll have to take that up with them. I do know you've made my life a little harder."

"How's that?"

"I'm going to catch a lot of grief for letting a fugitive hide a mile from where I sleep every night." He points to a two-story house just down the road. "I'm surprised my own dogs didn't flush him out."

I don't technically have a photographic memory, but I've consulted the map on my work cell enough to know his house is next on my list.

"Looks like I was going to come see you this evening either way," I say while palming the phone. "You want to get this out of the way?"

He checks his watch. "Can you do it in less than five minutes?"

I'm already tapping the screen as I answer in the affirmative. "What's your middle name, Mr. William Cody?"

"Robert."

"And how many people live at your house?"

"Just me and my wife."

He provides her name and their birthdates. Then I prepare for the less routine questions.

"These next questions are about race and ethnicity. Are either of you of Hispanic origin?"

"I'm not, but my wife is. She's Mexican American"

I continue nodding and tapping. "Now, for the 2025 Texas Census, Hispanic is an ethnicity and not a race, so you're both considered Caucasian."

He nods, checks his watch again.

"Just two more questions," I say, returning the phone to my back pocket, knowing I can remember his answer and record it after I get in my truck. "Do you both plan on remaining in The Republic for at least the next two years?"

"Absolutely. No better place on God's green earth."

I mumble in agreement. "And would you like to sponsor a family member's move from any other country?"

"No. We thought about having my mother-in-law come down from Durango, but she says she's fine."

"I bet. They say the Free State of Southwestern Colorado is basically the Wild Wild West. No rules. No taxes."

"No place for a woman in her eighties, you ask me. But I'm letting my wife handle that. It'll be a lot of immigration paperwork, but we can always bring her down later."

I nod and thank Buffalo Bill for his time, then close out his case in the cab of my dually.

Before starting my journey home, though, I let the darkness settle over me and wonder if folks are doing this in every other country across North America, helping count its current and prospective residents.

Preparing for the Future. That's the slogan for us Texas enumerators, printed right there on the back of our phone cases.

But I'm not fooled. I'm not readying for a new beginning.

I'm counting down to the end.

Rick Treon writes award-winning crime fiction depicting life and death in the Lone Star State. His debut thriller won the PenCraft Award for Literary Excellence in Suspense, and his Bartholomew Beck thriller series has garnered praise from bestsellers and industry reviewers alike. Lori Young will return in his upcoming novel, Divided States, set for release from Black Rose in June 2021.